FROM TUSCANY WITH LOVE

Recipes and Remembrances
of an Immigrant Child

LAURETTA AVINA

Copyright 2025 by MSI Press LLC

All rights reserved. No part of this book may be reproduced or utilized in any form or by any means, electronic or mechanical, including photocopying and recording, or by any information storage and retrieval system without permission in writing from the publisher.

For information, contact
MSI Press, LLC
1760-F Airline Hwy #203
Hollister, CA 95023

Copyeditor: Betty Lou Leaver

Front cover image: AI generated

Cover design & layout: Opeyemi Ikuborije

Photo credits: indicated on each photo

Recipe credits (as indicated in text): Annina Benassi, Mara Marsalla-Barsi Perez, Raylene Nunes, and Rose Rocchi

ISBN: 978-1-957354-63-7

Library of Congress Control Number: 2024952659

DEDICATION

This book is dedicated to the journey I have taken—not just through life, but also through memory, culture, and love. To the little girl I once was, who never stopped dreaming, never gave up on the beauty of her roots, and never lost sight of the importance of family.

CONTENTS

Dedication i

Acknowledgements. v

Introduction 3

Roots In Tuscany 5

New World In Gilroy 6

Navigating Elementary School 7

Struggles And Support 8

First Trauma In America 9

Adaptation And Isolation 10

Cultural Conflicts 11

Summers In Italy 12

Becoming American 13

In Retrospect 14

Befanini 19

Besciamella Sauce 27

Biscotti Soffici Di Zucchero 31

Bucellato Di Luccasweet Raisin Anise Bread 37

Carne Alla Pizzaiolasandwich Steaks Pizza Style 43

Castagnaccio—Torta Di Necci 49

Chicken Cacciatore With Polenta 55

Chicken Piccata 63

Chocolate Mousse Crown 69

Cialde 75

Cold Farro Salad 79

Crema Di Limoncello 85

Involtini Di Carne 89

Lasagna Alla Lucchese 95

Italian-Style Lentils 101

Ossi Di Morto 107

Osso Buco 113

Panettone Di Annina 119

Pasta, Aglio, Olio Di Oliva E Formaggio Parmesano 125

Pasta E Fagioli 131

Peperonata 137

Polpette (Meatballs) 143

Pomodori Ripieni Con Tonno 149

Rapini E Sasiccia Italiana 155

Risotto Con Funghi 161

Sformato String Bean Flan 167

Vellutata 175

About The Author 179

Select MSI Press LLC Publications 183

ACKNOWLEDGEMENTS

Writing *From Tuscany with Love* has been a journey of the heart, and I would not have completed it without the love, support, and guidance of so many.

To John, my incredible husband, for being my rock through it all. Your unwavering belief in me has given me the courage to keep going even when the path was difficult. For always supporting my crazy ideas, for your arms that are my sanctuary, thank you for being my partner in life and love.

To my mother, who patiently shared countless recipes, stories, and wisdom from our family's rich culinary traditions. Your influence is woven into every page of this book.

To Franca, my dear sister, I know you have guided me every step of the way from the heavens. You sent me signs when I needed them most, and your love has been a beacon of light. I owe this book, and so much of myself, to you.

To my sons, Isiah and Garrett, and my nephew, Andrew, thank you for giving my life purpose and meaning. You are my greatest joy, and this book is part of the legacy I leave for you.

To Dr. Betty Lou Leaver, for your inspiration, ideas, and guidance. Franca led me to you, and I truly believe I would not have completed this memoir without your gentle advice and support. Thank you for helping me shape my story into something beautiful.

To my family and friends, both here in the United States and beyond. Your love and connection to our shared heritage mean more to me than words can express. You have been a light in my life. Thank you for your support, laughter, and love. You have been part of my journey, and I am forever grateful.

Last, to the readers of this book, thank you for walking this path with me. I hope my story brings you a little closer to the love, flavors, and memories that make life so special.

Lauretta Avina

MEMORIES

FROM TUSCANY WITH LOVE

INTRODUCTION

Scenic photo of the famous Val D'Orcia in Tuscany
Courtesy of Francesco Ricca Lacomino (iStock)

In the tapestry of my life, there exists a thread of duality, a delicate interplay between the old world and the new, the familiar and the foreign. Born amid the sun-drenched hills of San Pancrazio, a tranquil village nestled in the heart of Tuscany, Italy, I was cradled in the warmth of tradition, heritage, and family love. Yet, fate had other plans for me: a journey that would traverse continents and cultures, shaping the very fabric of my being.

This is the story of my experience—a tale of resilience, perseverance, and the enduring power of the human spirit to transcend the boundaries of culture and circumstance. It is a story that speaks to the universal quest for belonging and the indomitable will to forge one's own path amid the chaos of change. Though my journey is far from over, I stand ready to face any new challenges that lie ahead, armed with the knowledge that within me beats the heart of two worlds, united in spirit.

ROOTS IN TUSCANY

It was my father's unwavering obsession with the American dream that uprooted our family from the *stradette* (small country roads) of our ancestral home and transplanted us to the bustling streets of Gilroy, California. Like a siren's call, the promise of America beckoned, casting its spell upon my father's soul and compelling him to seek fortune and opportunity in a land of boundless possibility.

My father's sister had moved to the USA (Gilroy) to help take care of my old paternal great uncle. She later married an older American Italian (Calabrese). My dad, in his great desire to move to this new land his sister now called home, pressured my aunt into sponsoring our move. In fact, my father was so enamored with the USA that when he first set foot on US soil, he kissed the ground.

This obsession was rooted in his experiences as a young boy during the German Nazi occupation of our village and many others throughout Italy during WWII. Even at a young age, he felt the depression, fear, and oppression the Germans imposed on the locals. It was rare for my father to share these childhood experiences with us, but I remember the joy he described when the Allied forces liberated Europe and eventually made their way to our little village. My father was in awe. The service members gave him chocolate and other treats, showing kindness and empathy that left an indelible mark on him. This experience planted the seed of his growing fascination with America.

NEW WORLD IN GILROY

When we moved to the USA, none of us spoke English. To most Americans, we sounded different, dressed differently, and our culture was foreign.

Many Americans based their perceptions of Italians on what they saw in movies like *The Godfather* or heard from their parents. This was 1972, and bigotry and racism were still very prevalent—not just toward Black people, but also toward the Irish, Mexicans, and Italians. I began to feel ashamed of being Italian and hated everything that made me "different."

Soon after we arrived in Gilroy, my parents bought a house built in the 1940s. Until then, we had been sharing housing with my great uncle, Romeo Paganucci, and my paternal aunt.

Our new house was a small three-bedroom, one-bath home with a tiny kitchen, a small dining area, and one family room. It had a large backyard overgrown with weeds. Looking back, I think of it as a small apartment for five people, with limited bathroom time. At the time, however, it felt like a palace; it just needed some love.

NAVIGATING ELEMENTARY SCHOOL

We moved into our new house, and to my mom's relief, there were many children of different ages on our block. She had a rosy picture in her head of us (my four-year-old sister, three-year-old brother, and me) making lots of friends and playing with them joyfully.

But making friends was challenging, especially when you didn't speak the language and were an Italian immigrant. Apart from the language barrier, we endured taunting and name-calling. The kids on the block called us derogatory names like "Dago" or "WOP."

Once I started learning English, I was told to "go back where you came from" and that we weren't wanted here. This was very hurtful and caused me to withdraw even more.

Constant reminders of how "strange" I was started to affect my self-confidence. Middle school and high school were the most challenging times for my social and emotional development. American culture conflicted with my Italian culture, and I craved belonging and acceptance. It felt crucial for me to assimilate—to learn the language, dress like American children, and adopt the "American" culture.

In school, teachers couldn't pronounce my name correctly, which embarrassed me. I hated the attention and the smirks from the other students. I remember wanting the earth to swallow me. Once, a teacher called me Veronica instead of Lauretta.

STRUGGLES AND SUPPORT

When I started school in Gilroy, I was ahead academically in math compared to the local students, but the language barrier was a significant hurdle. There was no bilingual education or assistance for Italian-speaking students at that time. I had to fail or succeed entirely on my own.

In Italy, I had successfully passed all my oral and written exams required for promotion to the next grade; I was going into the third grade. In Italy, school was six days a week and focused solely on academics, with breaks for recess and lunch.

The Glen View Elementary School administration placed me in second grade with Mrs. Rothamel, unsure of my academic skills. Once school started and I turned in my homework, especially math, it became clear that I belonged in third grade, so I was moved to Ms. Galletti's class. Ms. Galletti was American Italian and could speak a few words of Italian.

Two amazing American Italian women, Rose Rocchi and Raquel Moretti, helped translate my assignments. Rose became like a grandmother to me and a mother to my own mother, and her home became a second home for my family. Sadly, she has since passed away, and I miss her dearly. Rose's Italian, though not perfect, sounded like music to my ears.

These two angels came to my school for a few months, and when it became apparent that I was grasping English, their assistance was no longer needed. While most were amazed at how quickly I learned English, I was still very shy and worried about mispronouncing words. I avoided volunteering in class to avoid attention, knowing my grammar still needed improvement.

FIRST TRAUMA IN AMERICA

Unfortunately, soon after starting school, I experienced my first physical trauma at the hands of other students. A girl my age, whose name I prefer not to mention as the matter was eventually resolved, immediately became hostile toward me. She called me names and, at one point, challenged me to a fight.

Back home, I loved school. My best friends, Nino and Paolo often shared their homework with me before I was old enough to attend school. Their teacher even sent home assignments for me, which I eagerly completed. I always looked forward to school; my classmates were nice, and there were never any issues.

Now, everything was different. I struggled to adapt to a new school system and environment.

When this student singled me out as her victim, I was confused. I remember this first incident vividly, like a dream. Not fully understanding what I agreed to, I knew enough to meet this student across the street from the school after classes ended. Surrounded by other students, I was scared and nervous, unsure of what would happen next. The hitting began, and I defended myself. I could hear the kids encouraging the fight, at least that's what it sounded like. Thankfully, a parent drove by, saw what was happening, and broke up the fight. I remember her saying, "Go home," and we all did.

I made a new friend, Sonia, who lived a house away. Despite her mom initially forbidding her to hang out with me, we walked to school together for three years during elementary school and again during our freshman and sophomore years in high school. Sonia was smart and kind, with aspirations for a professional career. I vividly remember her dream of wearing a suit and carrying a briefcase.

Sonia helped me learn English correctly. One morning, walking to school, I said, "Close the light," and Sonia promptly corrected me, "Turn off the lights." This support, along with exposure to English at school and on TV, made me fluent in English within a year. While this was a positive development, it also meant I had to translate for my parents, which embarrassed me. As an adult now, I understand their reliance on me.

ADAPTATION AND ISOLATION

During my first year, I experienced taunting, name calling, and alienation from the kids at school and the ones who lived on my block. Yet, with each setback, I found within myself a reservoir of strength—a quiet determination to defy the limitations imposed by circumstance and carve out a space for myself in this brave new world.

Time passed. I made a few friends, but I never felt the same connection I had with my Italian classmates. I struggled to look and sound like the other students. I hated my name and secretly wished I could change it to something American like Barbara or Julie.

Because we were poor, my mom made some of my clothes. We shopped for clothes once a year at Mervyns in Salinas. I had no concept of a shopping mall until my senior year of high school. I had one pair of good shoes for school and one pair for every day. I got one pair of shoes, a winter jacket, and three dresses each year. My mom always dressed me in dresses.

Bullying continued on and off throughout elementary school and into junior high, becoming less frequent as my bullies grew tired of me. Beneath the veneer of hope and opportunity lay the stark reality of displacement and disconnection.

My father, a man with a chaotic mind, was a stranger to the tender affections of paternal love—a distant figure whose gaze was fixed upon the horizon of making a quick fortune, leaving scant room for the nurturing bonds of familial warmth to take root.

And so, amid the clamor of a new land, I found myself adrift, yearning for the comforting embrace of a home I lovingly remembered.

CULTURAL CONFLICTS

As I mentioned earlier, my Italian culture clashed with American culture. I have no memory of sleepovers and was rarely invited to parties. With my father's mental instability and irrational behavior, I was too embarrassed to bring friends home.

During middle school and the first three years of high school, I wasn't allowed to "hang out" at Taco Bell or Straw Hat with my peers. So, I was a bit of a recluse, and I was fine with that.

The only exception was drama class in high school and Gilroy Community Theatre. Surprisingly, I loved drama class and being in plays. I loved the close-knit feeling and bonding with other cast members. Plus, I loved the freedom of being someone other than myself.

Other than those couple of venues, all of my social life was contained within school walls. At home, I found comfort and escape in books and television. We had few TV channels, so I watched classics from the 1960s like *The Monkees, Lost in Space, I Love Lucy,* Saturday morning cartoons, *Leave It to Beaver, The Beverly Hillbillies, Bewitched, Star Trek, The Brady Bunch, The Addams Family,* and *The Mickey Mouse Club*. I also fell in love with old classic movies.

Amid the tumult of upheaval, I found pockets of solace—tiny oases of familiarity in the vast expanse of the unknown. Our little house nestled amid the sun-dappled streets of Gilroy became a sanctuary—a haven where I could hide and shut out the world.

But even when enveloped by the safety of home, the echoes of displacement and alienation reverberated through the corridors of my consciousness. As an immigrant navigating the treacherous waters of assimilation, I found myself caught between two worlds, struggling to reconcile the divergent strands of my identity with the relentless tide of societal prejudice and cultural dissonance.

SUMMERS IN ITALY

After five years in our adopted country, my parents sent me back to Italy for the whole summer. I was so elated I could barely stand it.

When I arrived, it felt like a sweet reunion of the heart and soul. Even though I was fairly young when I left, I clearly remembered how to walk, bicycle, or drive to all my relatives' homes and my elementary school. It felt like I had taken a trip back in time. Nothing seemed to have changed; to my eyes, everything was the same as when I left. The familiarity was soothing to my soul. Here, in my native country, I felt that I could truly be myself without the usual anxiety of trying to fit in and feel a sense of belonging. Here, I felt deep in my bones that I belonged.

My mother continued to send me to Italy every summer throughout high school, and I am not sure she fully understood just how much those summers meant to me. They became a refuge, a time to reconnect with myself and heal in ways I could not in California.

Those trips were not just good for my mental health; they also helped me deepen my bond with my Italian family, language, and culture. I reunited with old schoolmates and friends, strengthening my Italian and creating memories that tethered me to my roots. There was always so much to do for teenagers and young adults, and everything felt inclusive—family and friends all shared in the experience.

Back in Gilroy, options for my age group were limited. The few activities available often required money or a long drive, neither of which were always feasible. In Italy, the simplest joys—free and abundant—reminded me of what I missed most.

BECOMING AMERICAN

Upon my return to Gilroy, my parents soon took and passed their citizenship test. Because we children were under 18 at that time, we three became United States citizens when they did. Soon, I tucked my Italian passport away and from then on used my U.S. passport for all my future travels.

The years passed; I grew into an adult, but my love for my first home never dwindled. My feelings of shame turned into pride in being Italian. The gift of being able to still speak, read, and write Italian was priceless, and whereas once I never spoke Italian around non-family, I started to speak Italian more often around friends.

I also began to expose my friends to my culture, often having them over for an authentic Italian dinner, usually a five-course meal with foods that I grew up with. My friends loved coming over and experiencing the richness of my heritage through food. They started to ask me if I could make some of the dishes they had enjoyed at my house, which I happily provided. In true Italian fashion, food became the bridge and road to finally feeling a bit of peace and acceptance with what destiny had thrown my way.

These days, working in the Counseling Department of our town's high school, I often meet new immigrant students from various cultures—Mexican, Indian, Iranian, South Korean, to name a few that I recall. There are times when I share with these students that I was also an immigrant and started school not knowing English. I explain that I understand how they feel—the anxiety, confusion, frustration, loneliness, and fear. The emotion in their eyes is almost that of gratefulness, that someone like me was like them at one time. I have an extreme soft spot in my heart for these young immigrant children. I want to give them something that I did not receive. I want to wrap them in my arms and tell them that it is going to be all right.

Moving to a different country, at least in those days when my parents took that big step, was challenging, scary, confusing, and alienating. It is an experience that, if you are extra sensitive to your surroundings, I would not wish on you—or anyone

IN RETROSPECT

Photo credit: Peter Hermes Fuiran (iStock)

My journey from Tuscany to California was filled with challenges and triumphs. The initial years were marked by cultural conflicts, language barriers, and a constant struggle to fit in. Yet, these experiences also fostered resilience, adaptability, and a deep appreciation for my heritage.

The summers I spent in Italy as a teenager were a poignant reminder of where I came from and the unchanging beauty of my roots. It was a season of reconnection and self-discovery, reinforcing my identity and the sense of belonging that had been elusive in my early years in America.

As my family and I embraced our new life in the United States, we also carried with us the rich traditions and memories of our Italian heritage. My parents' successful citizenship journey symbolized our full integration into American society while maintaining the essence of who we are.

Reflecting on my past, I recognize the profound impact these experiences have had on shaping my character and outlook on life. My dual identity as an Italian American has enriched my life, offering me a unique perspective that blends the best of both worlds. Despite the challenges, I am grateful for the journey and the enduring connection to my first home, which continues to be a source of strength and inspiration. I now understand how fortunate I am, having lived and experienced two cultures. It is my belief that if people would learn more about other cultures, their minds would be more open and their tolerance of others greater. Like me, they might come to embrace and appreciate—and even cherish and value—the wonders that emerge from our marvelous differences.

FROM TUSCANY WITH LOVE

RECIPES

FROM TUSCANY WITH LOVE

BEFANINI

Photo by Lauretta Avina

FROM TUSCANY WITH LOVE

Befanini always conjure up the fondest memories of Christmas in Italy.

Christmas in Lucca is like stepping into a storybook where the cobblestone streets of this medieval Tuscan town come alive with warmth, tradition, and a touch of magic. The city, already rich with history, transforms into an enchanting holiday haven as December unfolds, wrapping its centuries-old walls in festive splendor.

Christmastime in Italy is magical. All the ancient and modern villages are decorated with lights and wrapped in Christmas cheer. From November 24th until after Epiphany, Piazza San Michele and Piazza Napoleone transform into a winter wonderland in Lucca. This bustling open market radiates the spirit of the holidays. These unique piazzas become small Christmas villages, complete with wooden cottages festooned in vibrant ribbons, twinkling lights, and festive wreaths. Statues of Santa Claus, playful elves, and glowing bows welcome visitors, drawing them into a world of seasonal delights.

Wooden stalls overflow with the irresistible bounty of Lucca's Christmas traditions. The rich aroma of roasted chestnuts, croccante (peanut brittle), hot chocolate, Buccellato, panettone, and mulled wine fill the air. You will also find tables filled with Befanini, handmade sweets, and bottles of craft beers and local wines from Lucca's surrounding hills. A feast for the senses, pine-scented air blends with wafts of coffee, candy, and warm chocolate, creating a smorgasbord of fragrances that makes your mouth salivate in anticipation of so many goodies to come.

Yet, Christmas in Lucca is more than just food; it is a celebration of art, craftsmanship, heritage, and entertainment. Smaller piazzas, like Piazza Citadels and Piazza de Cocomeri on Via di Poggio, offer havens for artisans. Knitters, carpenters, jewelers, and painters showcase their masterful work here. You'll find large, charming rag dolls and ceramics painted in vibrant hues in Piazza San Frediano, each piece unique and carefully crafted for the Christmas market of the Immaculate Conception.

All the while, entertainment delights visitors of all ages. Christmas pageants and shows bring joy and wonder to the town. Performances like "Un Canto di Natale" by the duo, La Dama e L'Unicorno, saturate the air with carols, enchanting both adults and children with music that echoes through the ancient streets. The piazzas and alleyways buzz with life as families, couples, and friends bundle up against the cold, laugh, sing, and engage in spirited conversation in a scene straight out of a Hallmark Christmas movie—minus the snow—filled with beauty, energy, and an undeniable sense of magic.

When I spent 2019 Christmas in Italy and visited the Christmas markets of Lucca, I felt transported to a place where time slowed, and smiles, joy and hope lingered in every corner. Decorations shimmered in the soft light, the music wove through the crisp winter air, and the warmth of the community enveloped me. I felt as if I were part of a Christmas Hallmark movie. I never wanted to leave this magical place—a Christmas dream made real in the heart of Tuscany.

In Lucca, Christmas blends nostalgia, tradition, and the quiet beauty of an Italian winter. The sensations linger in your heart long after the lights fade and the decorations are put away, a reminder of joyful memories made and the magic of home.

My only vibrant memory of Christmas in San Pancrazio was of Befana coming with her goodies. Because the Befana is an old witch, all she did was scare me into crying. I remember holding on tightly to my mom's neck while crying. Poor the Befana. I think I scared her more than she scared me.

Back during my young years in Italy, Santa Claus was less prevalent in Italian Culture than it is today. It was not as if we did not know who Babbo Natale (Santa) was, but in our culture, the gifts really came with the Befana on January 5th. Small gifts were exchanged on Christmas Eve, but the real event happened on January 5th.

Tuscan Befanini are made at Christmas time but are primarily made to celebrate the Befana. Legend states that the village women would bake Befanini so that she could snack on them during her deliveries on La Bafania, January 5; hence the name Befanini. These cookies are similar to American sugar cookies if a bit crunchier.

The Legend of La Befana

According to tradition, La Befana was a humble old woman who lived in a small, modest home during the time of Jesus Christ's birth. One evening, the Three Wise Men, on their journey to find the newborn Messiah, stopped at her house, seeking directions to Bethlehem along with food and shelter. Grateful for her hospitality and guidance, they invited La Befana to accompany them in their search for the Christ child.

At first, she declined, explaining that she had too many household chores to finish. However, later that night, an extraordinary, radiant light in the sky startled her awake. Interpreting it as a divine sign, La Befana regretted her decision and hurried to catch up with the Magi. Sadly, she lost her way and was never able to find the Wise Men or the baby Jesus.

Legend has it that every year, on the night of January 5th—the eve of the Feast of the Epiphany—La Befana sets off on her broomstick in search of the Christ child. She visits homes, leaving sweets and gifts for sleeping children, hoping that one of them might be the baby Jesus she has been seeking for so long.

One Italian Christmas and Befana tradition that my family has always followed, even in the United States, is that we do not put our Christmas tree away until after Epiphany; when the tree kings have brought their gifts to baby Jesus.

This timeless tale of La Befana has enchanted generations and continues to be celebrated year after year, keeping the magic and spirit of the season alive.

Photo credit: NGvozdeva (iStock)

Recipe for Befanini

Ingredients

For the dough:

    2 cups all-purpose flour

    ½ cup sugar

    8 ½ tablespoons butter, cut into small pieces

    1 teaspoon vanilla extract

    1 teaspoon baking powder

    1 egg

    1 tablespoon rum

    zest of 1 lemon

For the glazed topping:

    1 egg white

    colored sprinkles

Directions

1. Prepare the dough.

   - Preheat your oven to 350°F.
   - In a food processor, combine the butter, sugar, flour, and baking powder. Mix until the ingredients resemble fine crumbs.
   - Add the egg, vanilla extract, rum, and lemon zest.
   - Continue mixing until the dough comes together into a smooth ball.

2. Chill the dough.

   - Remove the dough from the food processor, shape it into a smooth ball, and flatten it slightly.
   - Wrap the dough in plastic wrap and refrigerate for one hour.

3. Roll and cut the cookies.

   - Allow the dough to sit for about ten minutes to soften slightly.
   - Lightly flour your work surface and roll the dough to about 1/8-inch thickness.
   - Use Christmas-themed cookie cutters to cut out shapes. Place the cookies onto a baking sheet.
   - Refrigerate the cut cookies for 30 minutes (no longer than one hour).

4. Add the glaze and sprinkles.

   - Beat the egg white lightly.
   - Use a pastry brush to glaze the cookies with the egg white, then sprinkle them generously with colored sprinkles.

5. Bake the cookies.

   - Bake in the preheated oven for 10-12 minutes, or until the cookies are pale brown (not dark).
   - Allow the cookies to cool completely before removing them from the baking sheet.

Enjoy your Befanini! Buon Natale e felice anno nuovo!

FROM TUSCANY WITH LOVE

BESCIAMELLA SAUCE

Photo by Lauretta Avina

FROM TUSCANY WITH LOVE

This creamy, Alfredo-like sauce is what my mom and I use in our *Lasagna alla Lucchese*, giving it the rich, smooth flavor that makes it so memorable. My curiosity about *Besciamella*—its origins and how it became so integral to Italian cuisine—has always pulled me deeper into exploring my family's strong ties to the history of Lucca.

It is well-known that the French, including Napoleon, spent considerable time in Italy, particularly in Lucca, Tuscany. In fact, there is a piazza named in his honor, *Piazza Napoleone,* inside the historic walls of Lucca. The French began their occupation of Lucca on July 9, 1800. Before that, Lucca was under Austrian control, following the War of the Second Coalition in 1799. Napoleon reversed the Austrian-established government upon his arrival from Egypt, and by 1805 he had made Lucca part of the *Principality of Lucca and Piombino. Napoleon placed his favorite* sister, Elisa Bonaparte Baciocchi, as governess of Lucca. Elisa also would end up becoming the Duchess of Lucca. She ruled from *Villa Reale* in Marlia, where my older cousin would later work as the head gardener for over 40 years.

With this historical backdrop, I dove deeper into the origins of *Besciamella* and found that its story is just as complex. The sauce was first mentioned in early 17th-century French cookbooks, and it became a favorite of the Duke of Orleans, who reportedly enjoyed it at nearly every meal. However, there's also some evidence that the roots of *Besciamella* trace back to Italy. Italian cookbook writer Bartolomeo Scappi mentioned a similar sauce in his *L'Opera*, published in 1570. Further, it's said that *Besciamella* may have been introduced to France by Catherine de' Medici, who brought many Italian recipes to the French court.

Italians originally referred to it as *salsa di colla*, meaning "glue sauce," for its use in binding pasta and vegetable dishes. This sauce is still essential in our *Lasagna alla Lucchese*, while southern regions of Italy, like Sicily and Calabria, often use ricotta, mozzarella, or spinach instead and, at times, add slices of hard-boiled eggs.

It is difficult to state with 100 percent certainty whether Besciamella is French or Italian although everything that I have read on Besciamella has me thinking that it leans toward French origins. In either case, *Besciamella* is a wonderful testament to the cultural exchange between Italy and France, woven into the history of my own hometown and cherished in the recipes passed down in my family.

Recipe for Besciamella Sauce

Ingredients

6 tablespoons of butter

1 tsp of nutmeg

3 - 4 tablespoons of flour

2 1/2 cup of whole milk

Directions

1. Heat.

   - In a saucepan, melt the butter over low heat. Stir one tablespoon of flour into the melted butter and, using a whisk, stir.
   - Keep adding one tablespoon of flour at a time.
   - Your sauce may start to get lumpy at this point, so add a bit of milk; whisk and repeat.
   - Do this until you have used all the flour and milk.

2. Thicken.

   - As the sauce starts to bubble, it should slowly start to thicken.
   - If you have been stirring for quite a while and the sauce is not thick enough, add more flour.
   - At the same time, add nutmeg.
   - Your sauce should be thick, similar to the consistency of Greek yogurt or sour cream.

   Ah, ready for use!

BISCOTTI SOFFICI DI ZUCCHERO

(Soft Sugar Cookies)

Recipe from Raylene Nunes

Photo credit: Raylene Nunes

FROM TUSCANY WITH LOVE

Over a decade ago, new neighbors moved in next to us. We met them one weekend while they were still settling in. Raylene, who's closer to my mother's age, and I clicked instantly. She is warm, friendly, and incredibly big-hearted. Raylene and her husband both retired from Hewlett-Packard, and at one time, they even owned a private plane. They have also travelled the world, and she has shown me many unique treasures from exotic faraway places. I have spent hours captivated by her stories; each one filled with wonder from the adventures they experienced.

Beyond her fascinating tales, Raylene has become a treasured mentor. I often turn to her for advice, particularly when it comes to decorating and crafting. She is creative, imaginative, smart, and always eager to share her knowledge. Over the years, she has gifted me beautiful crafting and decorating items, little treasures that inspire and remind me of her generosity.

Raylene is also a master in the kitchen; her cooking and baking are truly something to marvel at. I have tasted desserts and dishes she has prepared that left me in awe—not only of her talent but of the love she pours into everything she makes.

Because I have shared so much with her about this book, I felt inspired to include her in my story. Raylene has contributed so much to my life. Her presence on these pages feels like a way to honor the warmth and creativity she brings into my world.

The recipe that I am sharing has now become my favorite sugar cookies recipe. These cookies are soft, buttery, and taste like heaven in my mouth.

Recipe for Biscotti Soffici di Zucchero

Ingredients

3 cups all-purpose flour (for puffier cookies; use 2 3/4 cups for flatter cookies)

1/2 teaspoon baking soda

1/2 teaspoon baking powder

1/2 teaspoon salt

1/2 cup shortening

1 1/2 cups sugar

2 large eggs

1 cup sour cream

2 teaspoons pure vanilla extract (or 1 teaspoon for a milder vanilla flavor)

Directions

1. Prepare the dry ingredients:

    - In a medium bowl, whisk together the flour, baking soda, baking powder, and salt.
    - Set aside.

2. Cream the wet ingredients.

    - In another medium bowl (for this step use a hand-held electric mixer on medium-high speed to cream together the shortening, sugar, and eggs until the mixture is light and fluffy, about 1 to 1 1/2 minutes.
    - Scrape down the sides of the bowl constantly with a rubber spatula.

3. Add sour cream and vanilla.

    - Reduce the speed to low and then add the sour cream and vanilla extract.
    - Beat until fully combined, about 30 seconds.

6. Combine wet and dry ingredients.

    - Slowly add the flour mixture to the sour cream mixture in 2-3 increments, mixing until just combined. This should take about 1 to 1 1/2 minutes.
    - Cover the bowl with plastic wrap and refrigerate for 15-30 minutes. Do not refrigerate any longer.

7. Scoop and prepare for baking.

    - Line a 17 1/2" x 12 1/2" baking pan with parchment paper.
    - Working one pan at a time, use a 1 1/2" cookie scoop to drop balls of dough roughly 2 inches apart on the prepared pan, you can usually fit 15 per pan.
    - Refrigerate the pan of unbaked cookies for 15 minutes.

8. Bake the cookies.

    - Preheat the oven to 350°F (175°C).
    - Place the pan on the center rack and bake until the cookies are just set and barely browning around the edges, about 10 minutes.

9. Cool the cookies.

    - Remove the cookies from the oven.
    - Using a flat spatula, transfer the cookies to a wire rack or a large serving platter to cool completely.
    - Allow the cookies to cool completely before storing them.
    - Repeat the process until all the dough is baked.

    Now, display some patience and just wait until you can bite into them—or share them!

FROM TUSCANY WITH LOVE

BUCELLATO DI LUCCA
Sweet Raisin Anise Bread

Photo by Lauretta Avina

FROM TUSCANY WITH LOVE

This is one of my favorite sweet bread recipes. While it's not my own, it's a beloved sweet bread I've enjoyed for as long as I can remember.

This bread reminds me of walking down Via Fillunga toward Piazza San Michele in Lucca. The air there is fragrant with the sweet, licorice scent of baking Buccellato mingling with the rich aroma of espresso. The fragrance is so inviting and tempting that you can almost taste it. It is irresistible, compelling you to stop by one of the bakeries for a big slice to savor as you continue your walk or sit on the steps of San Michele in Foro, enjoying your Buccellato while watching the world go by.

The scent of baking Buccellato also brings up memories of fall and winter in my childhood in Gilroy. I remember walking home from school, entering the house, and being enveloped in the sweet smell of Buccellato. My taste buds would tingle with anticipation, eager to taste that sweet, yummy bread. I would close my eyes, and for a minute, the scent would transport me back to Lucca.

Buccellato has been a part of Lucca and its culture for thousands of years, dating back to the Romans. One old wives' tale claims that the Lucchesi believed the licorice flavor of the anise seeds held spiritual powers that could ward off evil spells. The smell and taste of freshly made Buccellato feels like a warm hug full of love.

Buccellato is also delicious, toasted with butter and jam and dunked in a caffe latte. I have also used slices of Buccellato instead of angel food or sponge cakes for other desserts. It adds a delicious, unique flavor to whatever dessert you choose to use it in.

You will find other versions of Buccellato, such as those in Sicily. Of course, I am biased, but, in my opinion, there is only one true Buccellato, the one from Lucca. As the old proverb says *Chi viene a Lucca e non mangia il Buccellato è come non ci fosse mai stato.* (Anyone who comes to Lucca and does not eat Buccellato is as if they have never been there).

Recipe for Bucellato di Lucca

Ingredients

1 package active dry yeast

1/2 cup warm water (110°F)

1 cup milk, at room temperature (or substitute with warm water)

3/4 cup sugar

4 Tbsp melted butter, at room temperature

1 1/2 cups raisins

About 6 cups all-purpose flour

2 heaping Tbsp anise seeds

1 tsp anise extract

1 large egg

Directions

1. Activate the yeast.

    - Add water, yeast, and a pinch of sugar in a large mixing bowl.
    - Stir to dissolve the yeast and sugar.
    - Add the egg, vanilla extract, rum, and lemon zest.
    - Let it sit for about 5 minutes until light foam forms on the surface.

2. Mix the ingredients.

    - Add the milk, anise extract, sugar, raisins, anise seeds, and melted butter to the yeast mixture and stir to combine.
    - Add flour gradually: Begin adding flour, a little at a time, mixing until the dough is thick but still sticky.

4. Knead the dough.

    - Transfer the dough onto a lightly floured surface and add the remaining flour gradually.
    - Knead until the dough forms a smooth, elastic ball that doesn't stick to your fingers.

5. First rise:

    - Place the dough back in the large bowl.
    - Cover the bowl with a cloth.
    - Let the dough rise in a warm place for 1-2 hours or until it has doubled in size.

6. Shape the loaves.

    - After the dough has risen, place it back on your flat surface and divide it into two equal parts.
    - Shape each half into a loaf.

6. Final rise.

    - Grease a baking sheet and place the loaves in the center.
    - Cover them with a cloth and let rise for another 30 minutes or until slightly puffed.
    - You can allow a longer rise if needed.

7. Preheat the oven.

    - Preheat your oven to 350°F (175°C).

8. Score and glaze.

    - Once the loaves have risen, score the bread on top with a sharp knife.
    - Beat the egg(s) and brush the egg wash over the loaves with a pastry brush to give them a glossy, golden-brown finish.

9. Bake.

    - Place the loaves in the preheated oven and bake for 35-45 minutes.
    - Using a toothpick, check the center to make sure it is done—if the toothpick comes out clean, the bread is ready.

10. Cool and serve.

- Allow the Buccellato to cool slightly.
- Then, slice.
- This flavorful Italian bread can be enjoyed warm from the oven, toasted with butter or peanut butter and jam, or even used to make French toast.

Enjoy it!

CARNE ALLA PIZZAIOLA
sandwich steaks pizza style

Photo credit: Debra Tibbs

FROM TUSCANY WITH LOVE

I am not particularly drawn to meat. There is something about the flavor of red meat that just does not sit well with me, with a couple of exceptions like filet mignon and BBQ tri-tip. However, the following dish is one exception I savor. Curious about its origins, I played detective during my trips back to Italy. A restaurant owner once told me this dish hails from Campania, a region near Naples. This is a traditional Italian meat course, il secondo piatto (the second course). But why is it considered the "second course" rather than the first?

In Italy, especially in my home region of Tuscany, we always begin with pasta for both lunch and dinner, yet unlike in the U.S., we never make pasta the main meal. Instead, a small serving is enjoyed alone, followed by the main dish, typically meat, along with a *contorno* or side dish, which might be vegetables, salad, or another light side. The goal is to savor each course without excess. Growing up, I found it surprising when dining in non-Italian homes that pasta would often be served as the entire meal, sometimes with salad and garlic bread on the side. And, interestingly, garlic bread is purely American—it's something you would rarely, if ever, see served in Italy.

Like spaghetti and meatballs, garlic bread emerged around the early 20th century during the wave of Italian immigration to America, loosely inspired by Italian bruschetta. Between 1870 and 1924, millions of Italians emigrated to the United States, searching for better opportunities. Southern Italy, in particular, faced severe poverty, especially in regions like Calabria, Sicily, and Mezzogiorno, the most impoverished areas at the time. High taxes and tariffs imposed by the northern Italian-dominated government, lack of arable land, deforestation, resource shortages, and recurring natural disasters spurred this migration. Interestingly, more Italians emigrated to South America than to the U.S.

Due to limited resources, many Italian immigrants were illiterate, especially compared to other European nations like France, Germany, and England. Most were farmers. Because of this, when they arrived at Ellis Island, many were assigned Americanized names; the officials, unfamiliar with Italian spellings, often simplified or replaced names with American equivalents.

In America, Italians discovered that many familiar ingredients—spices, wines, and olive oils—were scarce or unavailable. Some brought seeds to plant small gardens or, when they could, requested special items from relatives traveling to Italy. As resourceful Italians do, they adapted to what they had. Several dishes widely associated with Italian cuisine, like spaghetti and meatballs, garlic bread, pepperoni pizza, chicken parmesan, Caesar salad, and Italian dressing, were born from these adaptations rather than traditional Italian roots. For instance, in Italy, salads are typically dressed with simple oil and vinegar, never a creamy dressing.

Recipe for Carne alla Pizzaiola

Ingredients

1 lb. sandwich steaks (carne asada)

3-4 tbsp flour

4 tbsp olive oil

4 cloves California garlic, minced

1 cup shredded mozzarella

About 5 sage leaves, chopped

1/2 bunch fresh basil, chopped

6 fresh tomatoes, chopped (or one 14 oz can of tomatoes with juice)

Salt and pepper to taste

Directions

1. Prepare the steaks: Dredge the sandwich steaks in flour, coating them lightly on all sides.

2. Sear the steaks.

   - Heat the olive oil in a skillet over medium heat.
   - Cook the steaks for about 1 minute on each side until just browned.
   - Remove them from the skillet and set them aside on a plate.

3. Cook the sauce.

    - In the same skillet, add the chopped tomatoes and sage. Cook 3-4 minutes to allow the tomatoes to soften and release their juices.
    - Add Basil and Garlic: Stir in the chopped basil and garlic, cooking for another minute to infuse the flavors.

4. Simmer with steaks.

    - Return the steaks to the skillet, nestling them into the tomato mixture.
    - Cook covered on low heat for 15 to 20 minutes, letting the flavors meld.
    - A savory gravy should develop as it simmers.

5. Melt the Mozzarella.

    - Sprinkle the shredded mozzarella over the steaks.
    - Allow it to melt over low heat until gooey and entirely melted.

6. Serve.

    - Garnish with a sprinkle of oregano or fresh parsley for presentation and serve hot.

    Yes! Time for a very tasty dinner!

References

USA - Italian
Americans. https://www.globalsecurity.org/military/world/usa/people-italian.htm

Digital History. https://www.digitalhistory.uh.edu/voices/italian_immigration.cfm

FROM TUSCANY WITH LOVE

CASTAGNACCIO—TORTA DI NECCI

Photo of Castagnaccio by Lauretta Avina

FROM TUSCANY WITH LOVE

Ah, nothing brings back my Italian childhood memories like Castagnaccio or, as I remember it, Torta di Necci, made from chestnut flour! This is traditionally an autumn torte famous in Tuscany. It is an effortless and humble dessert, often called "the poor man's cake" because it has no butter, sugar, or eggs.

Back in the days of my grandparents and great-grandparents, chestnuts were the primary diet of farmers and peasants (along with Polenta). My memories are primarily from when I was a teenager and went to Italy often for the whole summer while on school break. My older cousin, with whom I stayed, used to make it for the family, and she would serve it with fresh homemade ricotta that she bought from a local farmer. I remember the flavors of chestnut, orange, and rosemary blending in with ricotta's natural sweetness and creaminess. It was such an explosion of flavors in my mouth. As I thought about it while writing this, my mouth was watering.

So, who does this recipe remind me of? It reminds me of my cousins, the Marchini, and the summers I stayed with them and enjoyed this delicious treat. But it also makes me think of my childhood friend, Roberto (Robertino), whom I have known since I was 13. Roberto is a fantastic cook, who constantly posts pictures on Facebook about all the excellent Italian meals he creates. Roberto likes to cook traditional recipes but sometimes adds his own twist. It was one such photo he posted on Facebook of *il Castagnaccio* that prompted me to reach out and ask him, "What is Castagnaccio?" When I was living there, I didn't remember it being called Castagnaccio, but Torta di Necci, so I didn't know what it was. When he explained it to me, of course, I knew. He promised to make me one next time I came to Italy, and he delivered on his promise, I'm sure sooner than he had imagined.

Imagine biting into a slice of Castagnaccio—the first flavor to hit your tastebuds is earthy and slightly nutty, with a hint of rosemary that lingers, beautifully offset by a subtle orange peel zest. Some describe its taste as "rustic," perhaps a touch austere, but therein lies its charm. As you savor each bite, the texture surprises you—soft, tender, almost like a fudgy embrace.

This rustic flavor transports me instantly to Tuscany: those green, undulating hills dotted with orderly olive groves, grapevines winding up their trellises, heavy with ripening fruit, and tall, stately cypress trees standing sentinel along the paths to countryside homes. The air there carries a sweet, spicy note from blossoming tiglio flowers, a fragrance as unique as Castagnaccio itself. Just the thought of it brings a smile to my face.

During the summer of 2022, I traveled to Italy to spend time with my relatives and continued to learn more about my culture. Living in the United States and being so focused on assimilating, I missed learning and experiencing many traditional Italian customs. My mom did her best to keep the ones that were possible to celebrate in the U.S., but not having access to some of the ingredients for traditional dishes made it difficult. My mom sometimes worked two jobs, so her time was limited. Besides, it's different from when you are living in Italy to fully appreciate the beauty and emotions felt while participating in all the various customs and holidays.

Anyway, I spent over five weeks in Italy, and it was during this trip that Roberto invited my aunt, my cousin and her husband, and me over for dinner. For dessert, Roberto asked me into his kitchen, and I watched him make the Castagnaccio.

My first cousin Michela, who is a wonderful cook herself and enjoys canning all of the many different types of vegetables and fruits that my uncle grows around their beautiful home and property in the small, mountainside village of Palleggio, which is located a bit north of Bagni di Lucca. Michela harvests chestnuts when the season begins and then takes them to a local flour mill and has the chestnuts turned into chestnut flour. Every time I visit, to my delight, I am always sent home with a nice size bag of her very special chestnut flour.

Recipe for Castagnaccio

Ingredients

400 g (14.11 oz) chestnut flour

500 g (17.64 oz) water

1/3 to 1/2 cup pine nuts (adjust to taste)

Peel of 1 orange, diced (remove as much of the white pith as possible)

1 sprig rosemary, fresh

About 1/2 cup extra virgin olive oil

Pinch of salt

Optional: 2 tablespoons sugar, a handful of raisins, and/or chopped walnuts

Instructions

1. Prepare the batter.

   - Sift the flour to eliminate lumps.
   - Add water and mix with a whisk until you obtain a nice creamy batter, like pancake batter. You do not want any lumps in your batter. You will find that you may need to add more water as the chestnut flower tends to absorb the water. If you must add more water, do so in small increments; you can always add more water.
   - Make sure to mix well.

2. Pour the batter into your pan.

   - I use a 14x4-inch tart pan.
   - Grease the bottom of your pan with a generous amount of olive oil.
   - After having greased your pan, pour in the batter.
   - At this point, you will arrange (on top) your orange pieces, rosemary sprig, and pine nuts. You do not need to be perfect; make sure that your ingredients are evenly distributed. Your batter is ready to be placed in the oven.
   - BUT one last step. Roberto taught me this: drizzle a generous amount of olive oil on top of the cake, around the edges of the batter. He drizzles in big circles. Roberto says not to be shy with the olive oil.

3. Bake and serve.

   - Place the pan in your pre-heated oven (350F degrees) and bake for 30- 35 minutes.
   - You can serve the Castagnaccio by itself or with ricotta.

   > *It is true, Castagnaccio may not be for everyone—*
   > *you may find its simplicity unusual for a dessert.*

   > *But I hope you will discover, as I have, the beauty*
   > *in its subtlety and savor each moment with it.*

FROM TUSCANY WITH LOVE

Chicken Cacciatore with Polenta

Photo of Chicken Cacciatore by Lauretta Avina

FROM TUSCANY WITH LOVE

Polenta, to me, always makes me think of the stories my mom shared with me about her growing up in Italy post WWII. Many people are not aware that Fascism was born in Italy during the early 20th century during WWI. Benito Mussolini gave his political movement the name *fascism* in 1919. Benito Mussolini together with Giovanni Gentile, an Italian intellectual, brought fascism to the mainstream and helped Mussolini write Mussolini's Fascist manifesto. According to Emmy Award winner Leslie Gornstein, who was a managing editor at CBS News, " It was because of Fascism that Benito Mussolini and Adolf Hitler, who, like many fascists, saw violence; violent revolution of governments, violent punishment of opponents, as key factors in fascism."

The root word for fascism is *fascio*, which means a bundle or group. With fascism, the meaning is "a bundle of people". Fascism was a political ideology that opposed liberalism, democracy, and Marxism, it embraced far-right ultranationalism, forcible suppression of any opposition, centralized autocracy, militarism, and subordination of any individual thought or interests. I found it amusing that during the Pandemic of 2020, the George Floyd riots, and in present times, the far-right, anti-vax and anti-science people kept blaming Antifa for all the ills taking place. Antifa means anti-fascism; I guess then I am guilty *along* with every single WWII allied veteran, the Resistenzia Italiana (Partisans), and anyone who embraces democracy.

As you can imagine, life for Italians under German occupation along with the Duce's Fascisti during WWII was full of fear, death, devastation, and starvation. Ordinary Italians did what they had to do to survive.

My maternal great-grandfather and grandfather, the family matriarchs, were farmers. They had orchards of fruit trees; cherry, peach, pears, and persimmons along with agricultural fields where they grew a plethora of vegetables. They also had farm animals such as cows, whose milk they used to make homemade butter. During the harvests, the family would sell their wares at farmer markets. This was how they made their living. They also grew grapes where both grandparents made homemade wine. Because the wine was considered sacred, my great-grandfather rarely sold the wine he made.

Like many other Italian towns during WWII, my hometown in Tuscany, was occupied by the Germans. Today, various monuments in my small town and surrounding villages remember those innocent civilians who were murdered by the Nazi Germans. One of the most famous Nazi massacre sites was at Sant'Anna di Stazzema, a small village in the mountains of Versilia, about 30 minutes' drive from my town and overlooking the oceanfront towns of Marina di Massa, and Forte di Marmi. Spike Lee's historical fiction movie, *The Miracle of St. Anna*, reenacts some real-life events that happened during WWII. One of them was Sant'Anna di Stazzema massacre.

For the first time in my life, I visited Sant'Anna di Stazzema during the summer of 2022, thanks to my "sister from another mother," Marisa, who is my second maternal cousin, and her wonderful husband, Marco. As I walked up to the now-famous chapel, where many victims' photos and memorabilia are displayed, I felt as though I was treading on hallowed ground.

The day was hot and humid, with not a single breeze, yet as I walked, I felt neither hot nor sweaty. An eerie silence palpated around me, overwhelming me with goosebumps, a sense of foreboding, and profound heartbreak. I tried to imagine myself in the victims' shoes, feeling their fear, hearing their prayers.

The two hours we spent at the site of this horrific massacre, carried out by Italian Fascists and German Nazis, left me utterly overwhelmed. The depth of cruelty and lack of humanity required to massacre women (some pregnant) and children is unfathomable.

Besides killing innocent civilians, one of the German Nazi's ways of making the locals submissive was to starve them. The continuing war left villages in ruins, making food scarce, and causing death by starvation. Thank goodness my maternal relatives were farmers. Although they had to be careful, they at least would not starve. One thing that both my great-grandfather and grandfather did build was a secret pantry within the walls of their home where they hid their olive oil, cheeses, grains, wine, and flour. Because the German Nazis would plunder and pillage each village they occupied, leaving the locals to starve, my grandfathers built this secret room to protect their food and staples. So, how does Polenta come into all of this? I am getting there, be patient.

My mother was born in January 1945, right before the end of the war. As post-war Italy worked to try and rebuild itself, for many Italians times were tough. My mom's family were poor farmers, who did not starve, but they barely got by. They lived in a large multigenerational, multistory farmhouse with no indoor plumbing or bathroom. The water was collected from the well located on the property. The outhouse was located far away from the house. When my mom was in elementary school, one of her chores was to collect water. In the wintertime, our area used to get very cold, and it would snow. The water in the well reached open air. Consequently, a layer of ice coated water. My mom would have to use her bare hands to break the ice, collect the water, and bring it inside. Goodness, we sure are spoiled nowadays!

One constant staple for meals was Polenta. My grandmother would cook one chicken, oftentimes cacciatore style as an example. My great-grandmother did not waste any parts of the chicken. With the neck and wings, my great-grandmother would make broth. With the liver and other organs, my grandmother would add that to her Sugo (aka spaghetti red meat sauce). My great-grandmother would cut the remainder of the cooked chicken's body into small pieces. This one chicken would feed a family of eight for lunch and dinner. Like a constant friend, Polenta was served at almost every meal. Leftover dinner Polenta was saved for the next day. Breakfast would consist of sliced Polenta, toasted in the fireplace, and if available, topped with some sugar. If sugar were not available, the Polenta would be dunked into warm milk and eaten that way. The family ate Polenta so often that my mom became sick and tired of it, but she ate it as it was better to eat it than go hungry.

When Polenta started being served in fancy restaurants, my mom made this comment, "It's hard to comprehend that Polenta is now considered gourmet. In my time it was a poor man's food, and it is what helped keep us from starving during and after WWII."

As for Chicken Cacciatore, the name *Cacciatore* in Italian means "hunter." This dish calls for mushrooms which an experienced hunter can easily find while trekking through the forests. Today, some of the forests of Tuscany are in natural parks. Still, the rolling hillsides are covered in woodlands, where mushrooms still thrive and where foraging for them is still a popular activity, especially in Autumn. At least, four edible kinds of mushrooms, prized by those in the culinary arts—porcini, chanterelles, black trumpets, and morels—cover the forests' floor. My maternal uncle Zio Beppino and my first cousin Michela, go foraging through the forest around their village in Palleggio, just above Bagni di Lucca, every fall. There are years that Porcini mushrooms can be found in the hundreds, nice and large. Then there are those years where finding Porcini mushrooms is challenging. Mother Nature controls the weather and the Porcini.

Recipe for Polenta with Chicken Cacciatore

Ingredients

1 frying chicken (4 lbs.)

½ cup of chianti wine

1/3 cup Olive Oil

2 cups of fresh, washed

2 cups of flour for coating chicken

sliced mushrooms

½ tbsp salt

¼ tsp of pepper

1 yellow onion, chopped

2 cloves of minced garlic

1 (14.5) can of diced tomatoes

2 tbsp of rosemary

½ cup of chopped olives. (I use Kalamata olives as I like how these olives› flavor blends with the tomato sauce).

Directions

1. Prepare the Polenta.

    ➤ Use any Polenta recipe; follow the instructions.

2. Prepare the chicken.

    ➤ Combine the flour, salt, and pepper in a plastic bag.
    ➤ Shake the chicken pieces in the flour mixture until they are evenly coated.
    ➤ Heat the oil in a large skillet with a cover or lid.
    ➤ Fry the chicken pieces until they are browned on both sides, then remove them from the skillet.

3. Prepare the vegetables.

> - In the same skillet, add the onion and garlic.
> - Sauté until the onion and garlic are slightly browned.
> - Return the chicken to the skillet and add the tomatoes, olives, rosemary, and wine.
> - Cover and simmer for 30 minutes over medium-low heat.
> - Add the mushrooms. Simmer for an additional 15 minutes.

References

Gornstein, L. (2020, October 20). *What is fascism? And what does it mean in 2020 America?* Cbsnews. Retrieved September 15, 2021 from https://www.cbsnews.com/news/what-is-fascism/.

Sant'Anna di Stazzema. Retrieved December 24, 2024 from www.santannadistazzema.org).

Sant'Anna di Stazzema and the Italian Resistance, Retrieved December 24, 2024 from https://www.visittuscany.com/en/ideas/santanna-di-stazzema-italian-resistance/.

FROM TUSCANY WITH LOVE

CHICKEN PICCATA

Photo credit: iStock

FROM TUSCANY WITH LOVE

My home in Italy was in the small *paese* (town) of San Pancrazio, which is about seven miles outside the walls of Lucca and next to Marlia. While I do not know when San Pancrazio was established, I did find some historical information about its church; this is the church where I took the sacrament of my first communion right before we left for the States. Scholars have concluded that the church in San Pancrazio dates to 983 and was completely rebuilt during the 12th century.

We lived in a duplex that held three townhomes, and we had the very bottom. The back side of this duplex was inside the grounds of Villa Oliva. In fact, my bedroom window overlooked the Villa Oliva grounds. I have memories of doing my homework while looking out the window at the beautifully manicured gardens.

The road that I took to walk to school was surrounded by rolling hills, vineyards, and agricultural fields. It was a magical walk with all of nature's beauty on display. It would also have me walking right past the church. San Pancrazio, when I lived there, was small, and everyone knew each other, along with the local children.

On days that we did not have school or during the summer months, I would spend time with my two best friends, Nino and Paolo, who happened to live right above our flat. We were the three musketeers. We would be gone from morning until we got hungry enough to come home. Our playground was the rolling hills, meadows, and heavily wooded areas that surrounded our town. We were explorers, and that is what we did: we explored. How we did not get into trouble or dangerous situations, I have no idea. One of the dangers we potentially faced was viper snakes. We did not care at that age as vipers never deterred or scared us enough to stay away from our "playground." We were free to play and explore to our hearts' content. This is my favorite part of my childhood. I was happy, carefree, and loved spending time with my friends. If I wanted to visit my grandparents, I could just walk there as they lived five minutes away. My great-grandparents lived about a 10-minute walk away. My other relatives were not that far away, and my friends were close, too. I felt safe and secure, in a little bubble of happiness.

So, what does all of this have to do with Chicken Piccata? Well, nothing really, except for Capers. Surrounding Villa Oliva is a tall, thick stone wall that is miles long and circles the villa and all its grounds. It is made of cement and rocks, and it is incredibly old. It is very tall, and unless one has a very tall ladder, no human could scale the wall, which was the point. The wall also connected to the outside (sides) of our building, and caper vines grew there. Caper vines are usually found in the Mediterranean, growing wild in dry stony areas. Something I did not know about capers but learned about while researching capers and how they grow is that capers are the unripe green flower buds. If left alone, these flower buds open to reveal white flowers.

On many occasions, my mom would ask me to go and pick some *capperi* (capers) for whatever dish she was going to prepare for lunch or dinner. I loved going to pick capers as it made me feel like a little helper. Ever since we moved to the states, using capers in my cooking transports me back to those times and those places, and it makes me smile.

Technically, chicken piccata is an Italian dish, but I have never eaten it at any point while living or visiting Italy. I have had the pleasure of eating out in many places in Tuscany, and I have never seen Chicken Piccata on a menu. I quizzed my relatives about this dish, and they, too, have never eaten it or heard about it. This might be a regional dish more popular in the Southern part of Italy. There are some theories that the true roots of this dish originated in France. This would make sense as the French were prominent in Italy for a long time. This started with the first French invasion of Italy in 1495 and, of course, Napoleon's invasion of Italy in 1796.

But we did have capers growing in our paese!

Recipe for Chicken Piccata

Ingredients

2 large skinless, boneless chicken breasts

4 Tbsp unsalted butter (if using salted butter, omit additional salt)

2 Tbsp fresh lemon juice

Pinch of salt (if using unsalted butter)

1/2 cup flour

3 Tbsp olive oil

4 garlic cloves, pressed

1/2 cup water

1/2 cup dry white wine (such as Pinot Grigio or Chardonnay)

2 Tbsp capers (or 1 Tbsp, if desired)

Garnish: chopped parsley and lemon wedges

Directions

1. Prepare the chicken.

    - Slice each chicken breast in half and crosswise to make four cutlets.
    - Pound each cutlet to about 1/2 inch thick.

2. Coat with flour.

    - Add flour to a gallon plastic bag (or a shallow bowl if you're avoiding plastic), then add the chicken cutlets.
    - Seal the bag and shake well or dip each piece in the bowl until the cutlets are well-coated with flour.

3. Sear the chicken.

    - Heat 2 tablespoons of olive oil in a large skillet over medium-high heat.
    - Add the chicken cutlets when the oil is hot and cook for about 2 minutes or until browned underneath. Flip the chicken and cook the other side for about 1 minute.
    - Transfer the partially cooked cutlets to a clean plate.

4. Sauté garlic and capers.

    - Add 1 tablespoon of olive oil to the skillet's oil. Add the garlic and cook, stirring often to avoid burning, for about 2 minutes.
    - Add the capers and white wine, swirling the skillet and scraping any browned bits from the bottom.
    - Allow the mixture to cook until most of the wine has evaporated, about 3 minutes.

5. Make the sauce.

    - Add the water and butter to the skillet.
    - Swirl the skillet vigorously to form an emulsion as the butter melts, about 2 minutes.

6. Finish cooking the chicken,

    - Return the chicken cutlets to the skillet.
    - Simmer until they are cooked through and the sauce has thickened slightly about 3-5 minutes.

7. Add lemon juice and garnish.

    - Turn off the heat and stir in the lemon juice.
    - Transfer the chicken to a platter.
    - Using a spoon, drizzle the sauce over the top of the chicken.
    - Garnish with chopped parsley and lemon wedges.

    Yum! Time to eat! Enjoy your meal!

CHOCOLATE MOUSSE CROWN

Recipe from Rose Rocchi

Photo by Lauretta Avina

FROM TUSCANY WITH LOVE

This dessert's name does not even hint at its magic. It is the richest, most indulgent mousse cake I have ever tasted. I would savor it daily if I could. If you love dark chocolate as I do, this dessert is pure, blissful decadence.

But I cannot take credit for this masterpiece. That honor goes to Rose Rocchi. Rose and her husband, Lawrence, were among the first friends we met when my family moved to Gilroy. My father had come ahead to find work, which he found with Lawrence. When we arrived, Rose and Lawrence welcomed us warmly, along with so many Italian Americans in Gilroy who shared our roots. Many of them spoke Italian from growing up with their immigrant parents, creating a feeling of home that wrapped us up in familiarity and comfort.

One of my most treasured memories is from the night before my wedding when Rose invited my sister, who was my maid of honor, and me to stay the night at her home. We would get ready for the wedding at Rose and Lawrence's house; her home essentially becoming the epicenter of all of the pre-wedding activities. The next morning, I expected a simple breakfast, but instead she had filled her long dining room table with a vibrant spread of Italian appetizers, side dishes, fruit, breads, and pastries. I stepped into the dining room that morning, overwhelmed by the sight—a feast lovingly prepared, a testament of care that left me speechless. There, for breakfast, also were my bridesmaids, relatives who had flown in from Italy for the wedding, my mother—and the photographer, taking photos.

Outside of my mother, no one had ever shown me such a depth of kindness. That morning became a memory I hold dearly, a reminder of Rose's enduring love and generosity.

Rose's passing left a deep ache in my heart, as if I'd lost a part of my cultural connection here in Gilroy. I miss her dearly, even now. Each time I make this chocolate mousse cake, I'm brought back to the moments I shared with this remarkable woman. Her warmth and spirit live on in every bite, making this recipe not just a dessert but a cherished part of my own story.

Recipe for Chocolate Mousse Crown

Ingredients

2/3 cup chocolate-flavored liqueur

1/2 cup cold water

1/4 cup sugar

2 cups heavy whipping cream, whipped

About 33 tubular cookies (such as Pepperidge Farm Pirouettes)

2 envelopes unflavored gelatin (Knox original)

2 2/3 cups semi-sweet chocolate chips

3 large eggs, separated

Directions

1. Prepare the gelatin mixture.
   - In a large saucepan, mix the chocolate liqueur with the cold water.
   - Sprinkle the gelatin over the top and let it stand for 1 minute.
   - Then, stir over low heat for about 3 minutes until the gelatin dissolves.

2. Melt the chocolate,
   - Add the chocolate chips to the saucepan and stir until melted.
   - Remove from heat.

3. Incorporate egg yolks.
   - Add the egg yolks, one at a time, to the chocolate mixture.
   - Beat well each time you add the egg.

4. Beat the egg whites.
   - In a separate large bowl, beat the egg whites until soft peaks form.
   - Gradually add the sugar and continue beating until glossy peaks form.

5. Combine mixtures.

    - Stir the beaten egg whites into the cooled chocolate mixture.
    - Then, gently fold in the whipped cream until thoroughly combined.

6. Prepare the springform pan.

    - Pour some of the mousse mixture into the bottom of a 9-inch springform pan.
    - This will help the Pirouette cookies stand better.

7. Line with cookies,

    - Carefully line the sides of the pan with the Pirouette cookies, standing them upright.
    - If the cookies are too long, you can snap off a bit from the top.
    - If they fall into the mixture, retrieve and place them back in position.

8. Fill the pan.

    - Fill the pan with the remaining mousse mixture.
    - Smooth the top.

9. Chill.

    - Cover the pan and place it in the refrigerator for at least 5 hours, preferably overnight.
    - This will allow the mousse to set.

10. Serve.

    - After chilling, remove the springform pan.
    - Decorate with whipped cream and your choice of fresh berries (such as strawberries or blueberries) or any other toppings you prefer.
    - Slice and serve your beautiful chocolate mousse cake!

This decadent dessert is sure to impress and is a delight for chocolate lovers. Enjoy!

FROM TUSCANY WITH LOVE

CIALDE

Italian Cialde also known as Pizelle

Photo by Lauretta Avina

FROM TUSCANY WITH LOVE

Italian Cialde is remarkably similar to Pizzelle. However, I had never heard of Pizzelle when I moved to the United States.

So, what are Cialde? Cialde (one is called a *cialda*) are delicious Tuscan artisanal dessert wafers. Cialde can be served in a variety of ways. They can be rolled and used to make cannoli. They can be served flat with a dusting of powdered sugar. You can stuff the rolled Cialda with ice cream, adding sliced strawberries and whipped cream on top of the wafer, like strawberry shortcake.

One of my favorite ways to eat Cialde is with Nutella. I love to spread Nutella on a warm cialde. The Nutella melts a bit, enhancing its creaminess. If you roll the cialde, you can fill them with ice cream, cannoli filling, or whipped cream and strawberries.

Cialde can be served in many ways; it just takes imagination. According to visittuscany.com, "They were invented in the 1920s by an innovative family of pastry chefs at a time when Montecatini was characterized exclusively by elite tourism. Today, cialde are known worldwide and are especially enjoyed when served with gelato and whipped cream or for a child's breakfast."

Cialde have become very popular and can be found at traditional festivals and street fairs. The original cialde are considered a symbol of Montecatini's cuisine.

Recipe for Cialde

Ingredients

1 cup sugar

1 egg

2 tsp vanilla extract

2 tbsp vegetable oil (or melted butter)

2 tbsp anise-flavored liqueur (such as Sambuca or Anisette)

2/3 cup water

1 1/2 cups flour

1 1/2 tsp anise seeds

1 tbsp olive oil (for brushing)

Directions

1. Preheat the Iron.

   ➤ Preheat your Pizzelle or waffle iron. If you do not have one, you can purchase one online, ranging from $39.99 to $200.00. Search for "Italian Pizzelle and waffle iron."

2. Prepare the Batter.

   ➤ In a larger bowl, combine all the ingredients except the anise seeds and flour.

   ➤ Beat well to blend.

   ➤ Stir in the anise seeds and flour, mixing just enough to blend. The batter should be a bit denser than pancake or crepe batter.

3. Cook the Cialde.

   ➤ If your iron is not nonstick, spray it with nonstick spray.

   ➤ Use a tablespoon or 1/4 cup to pour the batter onto the iron's round circle. Close the iron and wipe away any extra batter that seeps from the sides.

   ➤ Bake for 30-45 seconds until the cialde is a nice golden color.

   ➤ If you want to roll them, do so immediately after removing the cialde from the iron.

4. Serve and store.

   ➤ Serve the cialde as you wish.

   ➤ To freeze cialde, make sure that they are completely cool before storing.

   ➤ I would also suggest that you place a piece of plastic wrap in between the cialde before you freeze them.

   Yum, yum! Eat now or later! Take them to friends—or to a festival!

COLD FARRO SALAD

Photo credit: Jogy Abraham (iStock)

FROM TUSCANY WITH LOVE

I first tasted this wonderfully refreshing summer salad back in 1998 during lunch at my cousin Lorena's house. Summers in Italy are hot and humid, but this dish offers a cool, simple escape.

A bit about Lorena: she was my third cousin and closer in age to my parents, but to me, she was a friend and mentor in so many ways. Although Lorena has passed, the memories of our visits and her warmth remain close to my heart. She was short, as many Italian women are, but her spirit was immense. She had a heartfelt laugh and a reputation for exceptional cooking in the Marlia area. I'd call her a "Master Chef" without the formal title—she was a natural talent and well known for her delicious tordelli. Lorena's children, Mauro and Italo, along with Mauro's wife, Piera, now carry on her legacy at their restaurant, Le Colonne, perched in the Tuscan hills near Lucca, in a village called Matraia.

Le Colonne is reached by a winding road lined with olive groves, offering postcard-worthy views of Lucca and beyond. On a clear summer night, my cousin swears you can even see the coastline near Pisa in the distance. Under the stars, the lights below twinkle like scattered diamonds—a perfect backdrop for stargazing or for savoring a meal. Lorena's Tordelli helped secure Le Colonne as a must-visit.

Unlike classic Ravioli, which is traditionally cheese-filled, Tordelli is stuffed with beef or pork, Swiss chard, pine nuts, breadcrumbs, spices, and grated cheese. My great-grandmother even used rabbit meat when other options weren't available. While Ravioli is often described as meat-filled in broader culinary circles, in our corner of Tuscany, the distinction is clear: Ravioli is for cheese, and Tordelli is for meat.

As word spread that Lorena was making her famed Tordelli at Le Colonne, locals flocked to try them, sometimes forming lines waiting for tables. When Lorena grew older, she taught her daughter-in-law, Piera, to recreate her famous Tordelli and rich red Sugo so that her traditions would continue.

When I prepare this farro salad, memories of Lorena flood back to me, and I can almost hear her infectious laughter. Farro, a grain with a unique, nutty flavor, grows only in certain regions of Tuscany, Umbria and Abruzzo. Although it's also cultivated in parts of Germany, Austria, Switzerland, and the Middle East, Italian farro is often considered the gold standard. In my part of Tuscany, farro flourishes in the beautiful Garfagnana region, where it has been cultivated for centuries. This resilient grain thrives in Garfagnana's cool climate and high altitudes, making it a timeless staple of the area.

On a visit to my family in the summer of 2022, my first cousin, Michela, and her husband, Gennaro, took me on a scenic drive through Garfagnana, where we explored this beautiful region rich in history and natural beauty. One unforgettable stop was the ancient Verrucole Fortress, a castle originally built by the Gherardini family on even older human settlements. Dating back to the 10th and 13th centuries, the fortress is a powerful relic of a bygone era. Though it was closed to the public that day, we walked the grounds, gazing through the stone arches and peering into hidden nooks wherever we could. Standing there, I could easily imagine peasants bustling about their daily tasks within the fortress walls or noblewomen in elaborate dresses quietly stitching fine, intricate designs. The timelessness of the scene, surrounded by the enduring Garfagnana landscape, provided a vivid step back in time.

That day, my heart leaped as I laid eyes on golden fields cascading down the hillside, shimmering like gold under the sunlight. Mesmerized by their beauty, I asked Michela what these radiant fields were, and she told me they were farro, nearly ready for harvest. Standing there, surrounded by this natural splendor and centuries of history, a deep sense of pride for my homeland welled up within me. How could I ever have felt anything but reverence for my Italian heritage and culture in the face of such beauty and profound history? It was a moment that reconnected me to my roots, filling me with gratitude and awe.

Farro, celebrated for its high fiber and prebiotic qualities, makes a perfect base for refreshing summer salads and adds richness to winter soups. Whenever I buy it, I always check the label for "Product of Italy"—if it's not there, I won't buy it. Years ago, finding farro in American grocery stores was nearly impossible, but now it's easily available at my local market. I suppose this is one of the rare perks of globalization, bringing a cherished piece of my Italian heritage to my kitchen here.

Recipe for Col Farro Salad

Ingredients

1 package Italian farro

1 container fresh mozzarella, diced

5 slices prosciutto (or rosemary ham), diced into thicker pieces

1/2 to 1 bunch fresh basil, chopped

1/2 jar Giardiniera (Italian pickled vegetables), sliced into smaller pieces

1-2 jars capers, drained

Chopped Kalamata olives, to taste (about 1/2 jar, or adjust to preference)

Optional: 2 diced tomatoes

Directions

1. Cook the farro.

    - Follow the package instructions to cook the farro, adding a little salt to the water for
    - flavor.
    - Once cooked, drain any excess water and let the farro cool.
    - Drizzle with about 1/4
    - olive oil and toss well to coat.
    - Cover the bowl or pot and refrigerate to cool completely. I usually cook the farro the night before.

2. Prepare the ingredients while the farro cools.

    - Dice the fresh mozzarella.
    - Chop the prosciutto, basil, and Giardiniera.
    - Prepare the capers and olives.

3. Assemble the salad.

Once the farro has fully cooled, add the diced mozzarella, prosciutto, basil, Giardiniera, capers, and Kalamata olives to the bowl of farro.

4. Dress the salad.

- ➤ Drizzle about 1/4 cup of olive oil and add balsamic vinegar to taste,
- ➤ aiming for a balanced flavor where the vinegar complements but doesn't overpower.
- ➤ Add freshly ground black pepper and mix everything well with a large spoon.

5. Adjust seasoning.

- ➤ Taste the salad and adjust the seasonings as needed with additional salt, pepper, olive oil, or vinegar.

6. Refrigerate.

- ➤ Cover the bowl and refrigerate the salad for at least an hour or, ideally, overnight. Allowing it to rest helps the flavors blend beautifully.
- ➤ This Italian Farro Salad is best served chilled, making it a great make-ahead dish for gatherings or meals throughout the week.

Yes! Next week is taken care of!

LAURETTA AVINA

CREMA DI LIMONCELLO

(serve it chilled)

Photocredit: iStock

FROM TUSCANY WITH LOVE

Whenever I think of Limoncello, I'm reminded of my Zia Luciana, who's actually my second cousin but feels like a second mother, especially when I'm in Italy. She was the first person I knew who made her own Limoncello, inspiring me to start making it myself. There's also a special variation of this drink that brings her to mind: Crema di Limoncello—a creamy twist that's just as delicious and refreshing.

To give you a sense of who she is, my Zia Luciana could easily pass as my mom's twin. They look so much alike, and even their personalities are strikingly similar. Despite being first cousins, they're as close as sisters, talking on the phone every day. My zia is petite but has boundless energy, like my mom—always on the move, like the Energizer bunny. Much like my mom, Zia Luciana is always smiling. Whenever I'm in Italy, she fills the space my mom leaves behind, so I miss my mom a little less. These two are truly two peas in a pod! I love my Zia Luciana immensely.

Recipe for Crema di Limoncello

Ingredients

10 lemons

1 (750-ml) Everclear (this is what my aunt uses. I tend to use a high-end vodka)

8 cups (1.9 liters) whole milk

5 cups sugar (1 kilogram or 2.2 pounds)

1/2 vanilla bean, seeds, and pod or 2 vanilla sticks

Cheesecloth

Bottles

Directions

1. Prepare the lemon peel.

    - Wash the lemons well with a brush and then dry them.
    - Peel the lemons but be careful not to cut or peel the white flesh from the lemons. You only want the lemon peel. If you add too much of the white flesh, your Limoncello will taste bitter.

- Add the peels to a large pitcher, and then pour the alcohol inside the pitcher, completely submerging your lemon peels.
- Cover with plastic and let this sit for a minimum of one month in a cool and dark place; stir this every day.
- After about a month, the alcohol will have taken on a yellow color. This is an indication that the mix is ready for making Limoncello.

2. Make the limoncello.

- In a large pot, pour the milk and sugar.
- Over medium heat, stir until all the sugar is all dissolved and the mixture is hot but not yet boiling.
- Remove the pot from the burner and let it cool completely.
- Using your cheesecloth, strain the lemon mixture into the milk mixture, making sure to
- remove all the lemon zest/peels.
- Mix very well.
- Once it is cooled completely, pour the
- liquor into a bottle.
- You can store this in the freezer or refrigerator.

Now, you have something delicious to have on hand as needed/desired.

INVOLTINI DI CARNE

Photo credit: Webclipmaker (iStock)

FROM TUSCANY WITH LOVE

Without hesitation, this recipe makes me feel connected to my *Bisnonna* (Great-Grandmother) Cecilia. Although I was very young the last time I spent time with her, I can still picture her vividly. Like a traditional Italian Nonna, she pulled her grey hair neatly back in a bun and always dressed in a black dress, occasionally tying an apron around her waist. (After my Bisnonno Alfredo passed away, Bisnonna Cecilia followed the custom of her time and wore only black for the rest of her life.) Sadly, she passed two years after my great-grandfather did. I am convinced that when BisNonno passed away, Bisnonna felt as if part of her had died as well; they had been together for over 60 years.

I remember Bisnonna Cecilia as quiet and gentle, but my mom often shares stories of how strong-willed and resilient she was in her younger days—a true force to be reckoned with, a woman shaped by the harsh realities of her era. Born in 1884, she lived through two world wars, and times were incredibly challenging for most Italians during much of her lifetime.

During her era, Italy was struggling economically, lagging behind much of Europe. The country was primarily rural, with agriculture serving as the backbone of the economy. Farming techniques had barely evolved since the Middle Ages, infrastructure was poor, and poverty was widespread, particularly in southern Italy. Wealth was concentrated in the hands of a few large landowners, leaving many to work the land with little to show for labor. Italy was still a kingdom when Cecilia was born, known as "Il Regno d'Italia" (The Kingdom of Italy), established in 1861. It wasn't until 1946, after much civil unrest and discontent, that Italy became a republic.

My great-great-grandparents, great-grandparents, and grandparents were all farmers. They worked on land owned by the wealthy. My mother recalls that the landowner for whom my great-grandfather and grandfather worked was unusually kind. He allowed my family to live rent-free in a large farmhouse and only asked for half the profits from the produce and livestock they sold. He wanted half the harvest of peaches, pears, cherries, and grain but was uninterested in vegetables, pigs, or chickens. Despite these demands, the land was so bountiful that my family always had enough. Occasionally, the landowner would stop by and request a flask or two of homemade wine.

My mom taught me this recipe, which she learned from Bisnonna Cecilia. During hard times, when things like prosciutto were scarce, Bisnonna Cecilia would improvise with whatever was available. One of her simple techniques involved rolling the meat with a sprig of sage tucked inside and cooking it to perfection. Even in the simplest dishes, her creativity and resilience shone through, a testament to the resourcefulness of her time. Cooking this recipe always feels like a tribute to her strength and legacy, keeping her memory alive in my kitchen.

Recipe for Involtini di Carne

Ingredients

1 lb. sandwich steak

1-2 slices of prosciutto per steak

Salt and pepper to taste

Extra virgin olive oil

1 cup fresh sage, chopped

1 cup mushrooms (preferably porcini; reconstituted if dried)

3 cloves garlic, chopped (adjust to taste)

1/4 to 1/3 cup red wine (e.g., Burgundy)

Instructions

1. Prepare the meat.
    - Gently tenderize each sandwich steak with a meat tenderizer for a softer
    - texture.
    - Using a mezzaluna or food processor, finely chop the sage and garlic. Mix with salt and pepper to taste.

2. Fill and roll the steaks.
    - Lay 1-2 slices of prosciutto inside each steak.
    - Spread 1 teaspoon of the sage-garlic mixture on top of the prosciutto.
    - Roll the steak and secure it with a cooking string to hold its shape.
    - Repeat for all steaks.

3. Flour the rolls.

   ➤ Lightly dust each rolled steak with flour. This will help thicken the sauce during cooking.

4. Sear the rolls.

   ➤ Heat 1/3 cup EVOO in a large skillet over medium heat.

   ➤ Add the rolled steaks and sear until golden brown on all sides.

5. Add wine and mushrooms:

   ➤ Pour the red wine into the skillet and cook until it evaporates, allowing the meat to absorb the flavors.

   ➤ Add the mushrooms, stirring to combine with the meat and sauce.

6. Simmer and finish.

   ➤ Continue cooking over low heat for about 30 minutes, allowing the flavors to meld.

   ➤ The flour will combine with the meat juices and wine to create a rich, savory sauce.

7. Serve.

   ➤ Remove the cooking string before serving.

   ➤ Plate the rolled steaks and spoon the sauce over them.

   ➤ Pair with risotto, plain white rice, or crusty bread (such as Pugliese) for *scarpetta* to soak up the delicious sauce.

Buon Appetito!
This rustic dish embodies the heart of Italian comfort food,
perfect for sharing at the table with loved ones.

FROM TUSCANY WITH LOVE

LASAGNA ALLA LUCCHESE

Photo by Lauretta Avina

FROM TUSCANY WITH LOVE

One of the most fascinating—and, at times, amusing—experiences I had as a new immigrant in the U.S. was discovering American food. This account reflects my personal journey, and though I imagine other immigrants may have had similar experiences, I can only speak for myself.

To most Italians, American cuisine didn't have the best reputation. I recall family and friends, both in Italy and the U.S., commenting on the "strange" ways Americans cooked. They said the flavors were bland, that much of their meals came from cans, that casseroles were unappealing (casseroles were foreign to Italians), and that the pasta was overcooked. The meat sauce wasn't mixed with the pasta but poured directly from a jar onto spaghetti on a plate. Adding meat to pasta dishes, such as chicken in Fettuccine Alfredo, is not part of the Italian custom (at least not from my area). Most Italians that stated this had either traveled to the United States or had seen typical American meals on television. As these stories were shared, they were repeated and, of course, exaggerated.

When we moved to Gilroy, California, in June, the timing was perfect for summer barbecues, and local Italian American families welcomed us warmly with invitations to dinners and backyard cookouts. I'll never forget our first barbecue: chili beans, macaroni salad, and corn were served. All of these foods were new to us, especially corn. Wide-eyed and astonished, my mom whispered, "Why are they eating maize? We feed maize to the chickens back home!"

Despite our initial doubts, we tried everything and, to our surprise, found it all delicious. Huh! American food wasn't so bad after all. I was invited to a non-Italian friend's house for dinner a few times. I had what I'd call "authentic" American meals—and sometimes "American-style" Italian ones. I vividly remember one dinner: overcooked pasta (I watched in shock as my friend's mom rinsed the pasta in cold water after it was cooked) served "American-style" with meatballs on top. Where I'm from in Italy, we don't add meat or chicken to our pasta—just a flavorful sauce.

Other memorable dishes included fruit salad topped with marshmallows, Jello with whipped cream, soft white bread with no flavor (Wonder Bread!), and, most surprising of all, milk served at dinner. When I saw spaghetti and milk on the table together, I thought it must be a mistake! But, as my mom taught me, I didn't complain and politely tried everything except for the milk; I simply couldn't stomach milk with pasta.

Because money was very tight, my mom cooked all of our meals. Of course, they were mostly Italian dishes, so my exposure to American food was limited. There was a restaurant named Sambos in Gilroy back in the 1970s, and on your birthday, they would gift you a free hamburger-and-French-fries meal. This was a big deal to us children because we never went out to eat at fast food restaurants.

Over time, we became accustomed to the wide variety of American foods and enjoyed discovering new flavors. Many years later, my younger cousin from Italy visited and made a memorable comment: he loved the diverse foods here in the U.S.—Mexican, Chinese, Indian—dishes he had never tried before and was thrilled to experience. There are a few American foods that all my Italian relatives adore: hamburgers with French fries, bacon, beef jerky, and hot dogs. When my younger relatives visit us, the first places that they want to go out to eat at are In-and-Out Burger and, to my amusement, Taco Bell.

Italian cuisine can vary widely by region. Each region has its own specialties, with recipes reflecting local ingredients and culture. For example, Sicilian lasagna includes ricotta, mozzarella, and sometimes even hard-boiled eggs, which is much different from how lasagna would be made in Tuscany. Our Tuscan lasagna may not be as loaded as the Sicilian or Neapolitan versions, but it's no less delicious. Now, let me share my recipe for Lasagna alla Lucchese (from Lucca), which I promise will delight you as much as it has our family for generations.

Recipe for Lasagna alla Lucchese

Ingredients

1 box of dry lasagna noodles (or homemade pasta sheets)

1-2 jars of your favorite spaghetti sauce

Béchamel (Besciamella) sauce (see recipe in this book for preparation instructions)

Grated Parmesan cheese (enough to generously cover each layer)

Directions

1. Prepare the Lasagna noodles.

   - Cook one box of lasagna noodles according to the directions on the package. (Note: In general, Italians never rinse their pasta, and I believe that this has now caught on in society. The reason that the pasta is not rinsed is that the starch remains on the pasta, helping the sauce adhere to the pasta rather than slip off. This lasagna dish is one of the exceptions.)
   - Add a little oil to the water to prevent the noodles from sticking.
   - When the noodles are cooked, drain them, and rinse them off with cold water for handling them.

2. Prepare the baking dish.

   - Use a 9x13 oblong Pyrex baking dish.
   - Coat the bottom of the dish with nonstick spray.

3. Layer the Lasagna:

   - Bring the Besciamella, lasagna noodles, and spaghetti sauce close to your
   - working area.
   - Use two soup spoons: one for the Besciamella and one for the red sauce.
   - Layer the bottom of the dish with cooked lasagna noodles.
   - With a tablespoon, coat the noodles with Besciamella sauce.
   - Using the other spoon, spread the red sauce over the Besciamella. It is OK if the two sauces mix a bit.
   - Sprinkle Parmesan cheese over the red sauce, enough to lightly cover the noodles.
   - Repeat these steps until you have used all the noodles or reached the top of the dish.

4. Bake the Lasagna.

   - Preheat the oven to 350°F (175°C).
   - Bake the lasagna for about one hour until it is gently bubbling.

5. Rest and serve:

   - Let the lasagna cool and set for about 30 minutes before slicing to ensure the sauce is not runny.
   - For best results, refrigerate the lasagna overnight before serving.

   Enjoy your delicious Lasagna alla Lucchese!

ITALIAN-STYLE LENTILS

Photo credit: Julia Nagy (iStock)

FROM TUSCANY WITH LOVE

In Italy, especially in Tuscany, eating lentils for New Year's Eve or New Year's Day is a cherished tradition—though you can enjoy this dish anytime. From my research, I learned that this custom dates back to ancient Rome. Romans would exchange small leather pouches of lentils with friends and neighbors as New Year gifts, wishing each lentil would transform into a gold coin and bring prosperity. Thus, the more lentils you eat during the holiday, the more abundance and fortune you invite into the coming year.

This was a tradition I hadn't grown up with in the States, but when I spent Christmas with my family in Italy in December of 2019, I was reintroduced to it. My aunt, Zia Luciana, explained the tradition as she prepped for the evening's festivities. Lentils, she said, resemble small coins, and Italians believe that cooking them, so they plump and multiply symbolizes growing prosperity. The belief is that the more lentils you eat, the more luck, wealth, and success you'll have in the new year—or so the saying goes!

Recipe for Italian-Style Lentis

Ingredients

1 1/4 cups dried brown lentils, rinsed.

2 Tbsp olive oil

1 1/2 cups diced (medium size) carrots.

1 medium yellow onion, diced

4 cloves minced California garlic

4 (14.5 oz) cans vegetable broth

2 (14.5 oz) cans diced tomatoes

1 medium diced zucchini

2 cups packed chopped bietola (Italian Kale)

Salt and freshly ground black pepper

1 1/2 tsp dried basil

1/2 tsp dried oregano

1/2 tsp dried thyme

Parmesan cheese

Directions

1. Start with a large pot.

   - In the large pot, heat olive oil over medium-high heat.

2. Add, in order.

   - Add the diced onion and carrots, sauté for about 2 to 3 minutes.
   - Then add the minced garlic. Cook another 2 to 3 minutes; be careful not to burn the garlic.
   - Add the vegetable broth and canned, diced tomatoes.
   - Then add the lentils, thyme, basil, oregano, salt, and pepper (to taste). It is better to go lighter with the salt, you can always add more later if it needs it. I personally do not add any salt but that is just me.

3. Once the pot is boiling.

   - Reduce heat to medium/low for about 35 minutes; make sure to occasionally stir the pot.
   - Add the diced zucchini and the kale; continue cooking for about 15 minutes.
   - If you find that the lentils are starting to stick to the bottom of the pot because they have absorbed all the liquid, you can add more broth or water (about 1cup), I prefer using broth.

4. Taste the lentils to check for doneness.

   - Take a small teaspoon, cool it a bit, then taste.
   - If the lentils are tender to the bite, then they are done.
   - If you like your lentils much softer, then you will need to cook them longer.
   - There are varieties of lentils that, when cooked, have a firmer texture when eaten. It is honestly a personal preference.

5. Serve.

> Your lentils are done.

> The traditional way to serve them would be with rustic Italian bread and with a drizzle of olive oil over the lentils.

Enjoy and may the new year bring you good health and prosperity.
Buon Appetito e Buon Anno.

FROM TUSCANY WITH LOVE

LAURETTA AVINA

OSSI DI MORTO

Bones of the Dead

Photo credit: Jann Huizenga (iStock)

FROM TUSCANY WITH LOVE

These cookies are traditionally made for All Souls Day or Day of the Dead, which usually falls on November second. This tradition is very similar to the Mexican "Dias de los Muertos." As in the Mexican culture, Italians also visit and honor their deceased loves ones by visiting their graveside. Italians are known for having a customary treat for any celebration or holiday. In this case, Ossi di Morto are very appropriate. These cookies would also be appropriate to serve on Halloween. I remember Rose Rocchi making these cookies, but she made them round. They were delicious regardless of shape.

When I was a young child, these cookies kind of scared me just by their name. Their deliciousness was too good to pass up, however, so I put my fears aside and enjoyed them.

Recipe for Ossi di Morto

Ingredients

3 egg whites

1 3/4 cups flour (substitute with almond flour for a gluten-free option)

1/2 tsp baking powder

1 1/2 cups chopped almonds (roasted for extra flavor)

1/2 tsp grated lemon zest

1 tsp vanilla extract

1 tsp almond extract

1 3/4 cups sugar

Directions

1. Prepare the egg whites.

   - In a large mixing bowl, add egg whites and sugar.
   - Beat until stiff peaks form.

2. Incorporate flavorings.

    - Add the almond extract, lemon zest, vanilla extract and baking powder to the egg white mixture.
    - Beat lightly to combine.

3. Mix the dough.

    - Gradually fold in the flour and chopped almonds.
    - Mix with a whisk or beat lightly until the dough forms.

4. Shape the bones.

    - Lightly flour your hands. Take about 1 tablespoon of dough (more for larger bones) and roll it into a rope about 8 inches long and 3⁄4 inch thick.
    - Cut the rope into 3 pieces. Take one piece and roll it so that the center thins slightly and the ends remain thicker.
    - Gently press the center of each end with your finger to create a bone-like shape.
    - Repeat with the remaining dough.

5. Arrange on baking sheet.

    - Place the shaped cookies on a nonstick baking pan, ensuring they are slightly apart to prevent sticking.

6. Bake the cookies.

    - Preheat the oven to 375°F (190°C).
    - Bake the cookies for 10-12 minutes for a softer texture or up to 15 minutes for crispier cookies.

7. Cool and serve.

> - Remove the cookies from the oven.
> - Place them on a cookie rack and allow them to cool completely.
> - *Serving tip*: These cookies pair beautifully with espresso, hot tea, or a festive beverage.
>
>   *The unique bone shape makes these cookies a conversation piece for gatherings or celebrations.*

FROM TUSCANY WITH LOVE

LAURETTA AVINA

OSSO BUCO

recipe by Mara Marsalla-Barsi Perez (my mom)

Photo credit: Vladimir Mironov (iStock)

FROM TUSCANY WITH LOVE

In my readings, I learned that Osso Buco originated from the culinary traditions of Northern Italy though there is no exact timeline for its invention. It is believed to have emerged sometime between 1800 and 1900. There are two versions of Osso Buco—the modern version with tomatoes and Osso Buco in Bianco (white Osso Buco), flavored with cinnamon, bay leaves, and gremolata.

During the medieval era, Northern Italy, particularly Milan, was renowned for its culinary scene. Milan was the main hub for trade and commerce, and chefs in Milan and the surrounding areas became famous for their new and inventive ways to celebrate local cuisine. They reveled in the variety of unique spices, ingredients, and different cooking methods brought by trade from around the world. Chefs would gather and share their culinary knowledge. It is theorized that these gatherings laid the foundation for Osso Buco.

Osso Buco's flavor is a marriage of tender veal shanks, fragrant vegetables, rich tomato-based sauce, and fresh herbs. This is my mother's recipe for Osso Buco.

Recipe for Osso Buco

Ingredients

Veal Shanks: 6 lbs., cut into 2-inch pieces

Vegetables:

1 1/2 cups chopped onion

1/2 cup celery, chopped

1/2 cup carrots, chopped

1 clove garlic, minced

Liquids:

1/2 cup olive oil

1/2 cup white wine

1 (24 oz) can of tomatoes (crushed or diced)

13 3/4 oz chicken broth

Seasonings:

- 1 tbsp salt
- 1/2 tsp sweet basil
- 1/4 tsp pepper
- 2 bay leaves
- 1 tbsp grated lemon peel
- 2 tbsp chopped parsley

Directions

1. Brown the veal.

    - Heat olive oil in a Dutch oven over medium-high heat.
    - Brown the veal shanks on both sides until golden.
    - Remove and set aside in a large bowl.

2. Cook the vegetables.

    - In the same pot, sauté onions, celery, carrots, and garlic until they are softened and fragrant.

3. Combine the ingredients.

    - Return the veal shanks to the pot.
    - Dice the tomatoes and add them, along with their juices, to the pan.

4. Braise.

    - Cover the Dutch oven and simmer the mixture on low heat for 1 1/2 to 2 hours or until the veal is tender and begins to pull away from the bone.

5. Add final ingredients.

    - Once the veal is tender, stir in the chicken broth, white wine, salt, sweet basil, pepper, and bay leaves.
    - Simmer gently for a few minutes to meld the flavors.

6. Serve and garnish.

    - Transfer the osso buco to a serving platter and spoon the sauce over the top.
    - Garnish with the chopped parsley and grated lemon peel for a bright and aromatic finish.
    - *Serving suggestions*: This dish pairs beautifully with Risotto alla Milanese, plain white rice, or crusty bread to soak up the flavorful sauce.

FROM TUSCANY WITH LOVE

PANETTONE DI ANNINA

Panettone by Annina Benassi

Photo credit: Funebre (iStock)

FROM TUSCANY WITH LOVE

Panettone may be a holiday staple, but it has never been my go-to holiday treat. I prefer Pandoro. Yet, there was one panettone I could not resist, one that tasted worlds away from anything store-bought: Annina's homemade panettone.

When my family arrived in Gilroy, the local Italian community embraced us with open arms. One couple, Asperio and Annina Benassi, became especially close. They had immigrated to the U.S. from Garfagnana in Tuscany during the great migration and, like many Italians, had settled on a plot of land to farm prunes. Over time, Asperio and Annina became like family, joining us for countless meals and celebrations. Annina had a warm, generous spirit and was full of stories about her life in Italy. Listening to her share memories of the old country felt like getting a personal crossing through time and receiving history lessons over cups of espresso.

Unfortunately, we did not get to spend many years with Asperio as he passed away a few years after we arrived. Annina and my mother became dear friends, and Annina often dropped in just to spend time with my mom. Because Annina only had sons, I feel that my mom became the surrogate daughter Annina never had. When Annina passed away, like Rose before her, and a few other close friends from the Italian community, it felt as though a piece of my world had shifted. I missed their company, the laughter, and, of course, the long hours around the dinner table, sharing food and stories.

One of my sweetest memories of Annina was her panettone. She made it from scratch, and no one has ever made it like she did. She knew I loved it, so every so often, she would surprise me with one. Her panettone was soft, fresh, and perfectly balanced with raisins and candied fruit. Taking a bite of her panettone brought me right back to Christmas time in Italy, filling me with nostalgia and warmth.

I remember one evening, I cozied up with holiday Hallmark movies, I took the panettone and sat on the sofa and savored however much I wanted. I felt no guilt—just the comfort and joy of a truly special treat and of course, thought of Annina.

To this day, no one makes panettone like Annina did. It was more than just a dessert to me; it was a connection to her, to Italy, and to so many wonderful memories. She is deeply missed, and each holiday season, I remember her gift of panettone and all the love she put into it.

Recipe for Panettone di Annina

Ingredients

(all ingredients should be at room temperature)

6 cups all-purpose flour

1 cup sugar

1 tsp anise extract

1 tsp salt

2 envelopes of dry yeast

4 eggs, beaten

3/4 cup butter, softened

1 cup room warm water

3/4 cup candied fruit, chopped

1/4 cup pine nuts

3/4 cup raisins

Directions

1. Prepare the dough base.

    - In a small bowl, dissolve the yeast in 1 cup of warm water.
    - Beat the eggs in a large mixing bowl; add the melted butter and stir well to combine.
    - Slowly, add the dry ingredients: flour, sugar, anise extract, and salt into the egg and
    - butter mixture. Mix well.
    - Once all the ingredients have been mixed, cover the bowl and place it in a warm

- place until the dough doubles in size.
- Once the dough has risen, punch it down, then add the raisins, candied fruit, and pine
- nuts, kneading until the fruits and nuts are evenly mixed into the dough.

2. Shape the Dough and second rise.

- Divide the dough into half and place each in a greased 8-inch round tin.
- Mold the dough to fit the tins.
- Cover the tins and let them rise again until doubled in size.
- 3. Egg wash and bake.
- Beat 1-2 eggs with 1 teaspoon of water to create an egg wash.
- Once the dough has doubled in size, brush the tops with the egg wash.
- Bake in the oven at 325 degrees for 35-40 minutes, or until the bread is golden brown.

Thank you, Annina, for such delicious Panettone!

FROM TUSCANY WITH LOVE

LAURETTA AVINA

PASTA, AGLIO, OLIO DI OLIVA E FORMAGGIO PARMESANO

Pasta with garlic, olive oil and parmesan cheese

Photo credit: Lauri Patterson (iStock)

FROM TUSCANY WITH LOVE

This dish reminds me of my school days in Italy. The aroma of this simple yet very flavorful dish brings me back to those early years in school in San Pancrazio. Back then, the elementary school's schedule was a bit different. We went to school six days a week, with Sundays off. We attended school until 1:00 p.m. with a 15-minute snack break. When I arrived home after school, I was usually hungry and ready to eat lunch. On many occasions, when the cupboards were bare, my mom would make this dish for me because it was simple and required few ingredients.

I also feel that this recipe helped me win the Miss Gilroy Garlic Festival pageant in 1983. On that day, the first step of the competition was the judges' interview. This category also awarded the most points, and it provided the judges with their first impression of the contestant. I knew it was important to be on point, and the funny thing is that I was not nervous.

The time of the interview arrived, and I entered the interview room. Seated at a long table was the panel of five judges (I think there were five judges; it had to be an odd number). I sat down in the chair, strategically placed facing the judges and in the middle of the panel and waited to be interviewed. After some pleasantries, the questions started. Each judge asked a question. One question and my answer, I felt, made me stand out to the judges from the other contestants. I have since judged many pageants at the local and state levels, so I am fully aware now of the importance of the judges' interview. The impact a contestant makes on the judges usually stays with them throughout the whole program, and it is challenging not to be biased.

The question was, "What is your favorite garlic dish to eat?" Without hesitating and with confidence, I answered. I explained about my early childhood in Italy and how my mom would make this dish (I explained what it was) when I arrived home from school. The judges were intrigued and proceeded to ask me how it was cooked. I explained. I remember the positivity that I felt as I engaged with the judges.

Once the interview was completed and I left, I sat in my car with butterflies in my stomach. I felt positive energy from the judges; they had really engaged with me, and all this made me feel good and confident. I was on cloud nine. That confident and happy feeling stayed with me during the evening program of the pageant, influencing my performance.

That evening, I won the pageant and was crowned Miss Gilroy Garlic Queen 1983. In my heart, I knew the interview and my connection to the judges had a profound influence on the voting.

Recipe for Pasta, Aglio, Olio di Oliva e Formaggio Parmesano

Ingredients

1 lb. spaghetti (serves 4)

6 cloves California garlic, minced or chopped

1/2 cup Parmesan cheese (adjust to taste)

1/2 cup olive oil

Salt to taste

Optional: Red pepper flakes or fresh parsley for garnish

Directions

1. Cook the spaghetti.

   - In a large pot, add water and a pinch of salt.
   - Bring the water to boil.
   - Once the water is boiling, add the spaghetti to the water and cook it until the pasta is al dente. Use the directions on the package for guidance on timing.
   - Strain the cooked pasta but reserve about 1 cup of pasta water. I usually take a ladle before I drain the pasta and add the pasta water to a bowl.

2. Prepare the garlic.

   - In a large skillet, heat the olive oil over medium heat.
   - Add the minced garlic and cook gently, stirring constantly, until it becomes fragrant and lightly golden (about 2 minutes). Be careful not to burn the garlic.

3. Combine the ingredients.

    ➤ Take the spaghetti pasta, add it to the skillet and toss with the garlic and olive oil. Add a couple of tablespoons of pasta water and mix well to coat the pasta.

    ➤ Now add the parmesan cheese, toss again really well.

    ➤ You can add more pasta water if you feel the spaghetti looks too dry.

4. Season and garnish.

    ➤ Sprinkle red pepper flakes or chopped parsley on top. This is optional

5. Serve immediately

    ➤ Plate the pasta.

    ➤ Serve with extra Parmesan cheese on the side for those who want more.

    ➤ *Tips:* (1) You can add some zing by adding some lemon juice or zest. This can also add some color to brighten the dish. (2) Pair this classic dish with chicken or pork, some crusty bread and a simple salad for a complete meal.

    With or without that extra cheese, sooooo delicious!

FROM TUSCANY WITH LOVE

PASTA E FAGIOLI

Pasta and Beans

Photo by Lauretta Avina

FROM TUSCANY WITH LOVE

Pasta e fagioli instantly reminds me of chilly winter days, holiday gatherings, and a fireplace crackling with fire, warm and cozy. To me, this dish is pure comfort—a warm, hearty bowl that nourishes the soul as much as the body.

Whenever we make ravioli, there is usually a bit of dough left over which I roll into fettuccine to use for my Pasta e Fagioli. While the dish is delicious with any pasta, using homemade pasta elevates it to a level store-bought cannot quite reach. This classic recipe is both budget-friendly and filling, traditionally known as *il piatto dei poveri* (the poor man's

dish) in Italy. Dean Martin even immortalized it in his song "That's Amore," singing, "When the stars make you drool, just like pasta fazool, that's amore." While *fazoo*" isn't the grammatically correct word for fagioli, it's a slang word commonly used in Naples and Calabria, adding a regional touch to the song's charm.

I eat Pasta e Fagioli topped with a generous pour of olive oil and freshly grated parmesan cheese.

Recipe for Pasta e Fagioli

Ingredients

4 cups chicken or vegetable broth

3 cloves garlic, chopped

1 or 2 cans (15 1/2 oz each) of cannellini beans (or preferred beans)

1/2 teaspoon salt

2 cups homemade fettuccine or ditalini pasta (store-bought is fine if needed)

1 cup diced tomatoes (optional)

1/4 teaspoon oregano

1/4 teaspoon pepper

1 teaspoon salt

1 onion, chopped

1 cup chopped Italian kale (optional)

Directions

1. Prepare the broth and beans.

   - Heat the broth in a large pot until it begins to boil.
   - Add the beans and reduce the heat to a simmer.

2. Sauté the vegetables.

   - In a separate skillet, add a drizzle of olive oil to coat the pan.
   - Sauté the onion, garlic, and tomatoes for about 1 minute, being careful not to burn the garlic.
   - Add the kale and cook for an additional 2 minutes, until it starts to soften.

3. Combine and simmer.

   - Transfer the sautéed vegetables and kale into the pot with the beans.
   - Add the oregano, pepper, and salt.
   - Let the mixture gently simmer for about 20 minutes to allow the flavors to meld.

4. Add the pasta.

   - Add the pasta.
   - Let it simmer for an additional 10 minutes or until the pasta is done. Note: homemade pasta will cook faster, so adjust timing as needed.

5. Adjust and serve.

   - Taste the soup and add more salt or seasoning if needed.
   - Serve warm.
   - The traditional way to eat this dish is topped with olive oil and freshly grated Parmesan cheese.

➤ Feel free to use canned tomatoes or personalize it with different herbs and seasoning. Some individuals use jarred store-bought spaghetti sauce rather than tomatoes. (I have also made this without tomatoes and it is just as delicious.) I do not like to use the store-bought spaghetti sauce it has added sugars and tastes too sweet for my palate.

I hope you enjoy this easy and adaptable dish.

PEPERONATA

Photo by Lauretta Avina

FROM TUSCANY WITH LOVE

This recipe doesn't remind me of anyone specific, but I do want to share a funny story related to it, involving bell peppers.

When we first arrived in the U.S., we were exposed to various American foods we had never tasted before—hot dogs, corn on the cob, cornbread, hamburgers, chili, and American-style pizza. We also noticed certain Italian words used in advertising that caught our attention. One such word was *sale*, which in Italian means "salt." We wondered why there was such a need for salt, as "Sale" signs were everywhere! Finally, my mom asked my aunt, who explained what it actually meant in English, and we all had a good laugh.

Another word that particularly caught my ear was *pepperoni*. In Italian, *peperoni* mean bell peppers (plural). "Wow," I thought. "Americans must really love bell peppers!" Eventually, I learned that *pepperoni* (English) is not the same as *peperoni* (Italian). It's actually a type of salami mainly used as a pizza topping. I had never heard of this kind of salami before, and I couldn't help but laugh to myself, realizing all those months I thought Americans had a love affair with bell peppers.

Growing up in a household where we rarely ate out, and certainly not at fast-food restaurants, these foods were completely foreign to me. Even now, in Italy, pepperoni as a pizza topping is unheard of, at least in my region. I've never

seen it at any pizzeria in Tuscany.

Now, let's get back to the recipe. I love Peperonata, especially in the summer when our tomatoes are at their ripest. It has a sweet, mildly tangy flavor, and it's so simple to make. I've seen recipes that call for tomato sauce, but fresh tomatoes are the best. Some recipes add sugar, vinegar, or garlic, but trust me, you don't need all that. The simplicity of this

recipe surprises people because it's so flavorful. One neat thing about Peperonata is its versatility. I've used zucchini and green beans in place of bell peppers, and while the taste is slightly different, it's just as delicious.

Recipe for Peperonata

Ingredients

1 pound of green bell peppers (you can use yellow or red bell peppers; I prefer the flavor of the green ones) sliced

1 large yellow onion, thinly sliced

1 pound of fresh tomatoes, chopped or 1 to 2 cans of diced tomatoes

2-3 cloves of garlic, chopped or minced. (this is optional)

1/4 to 1/3 cup tablespoons of olive oil

Salt and pepper to taste

Instructions

1. Heat the olive oil.

   - Turn on your stovetop/flame to medium.
   - Add the olive oil to a large skillet and allow it to warm up for a few seconds.

2. Add the onions and garlic.

   - Add the minced garlic and sliced onions to the skillet.
   - Let them sauté for about 5 minutes until the ingredients are soft and fragrant, being sure not to burn the garlic.

3. Add the bell peppers.

   - At this point, you will add the sliced bell peppers.
   - Continue cooking for another 5 minutes or until the bell peppers are starting to soften.

3. Add the tomatoes.

   - Add your chopped or canned tomatoes.
   - Stir all of the ingredients well.

4. Bring to a simmer.

    - Increase your flame/stovetop heat setting and let your ingredients come to a gentle simmer.
    - Keep stirring to blend all your veggies well.

5. Simmer for 5 minutes.

    - Cover the Peperonata and simmer uncovered for about 5 minutes.
    - Keep stirring to ensure that everything is well combined and does not stick to the skillet.

6. Lower the heat and cover.

    - After about 5 minutes, reduce the flame/stovetop to low.
    - Cover the skillet and let it simmer for about 40 min.
    - Be sure to occasionally stir.
    - The tomatoes, bell peppers, onions, and garlic will have created a nice, juicy, rich sauce.
    - If after 30 minutes, there is still a lot of juice, remove the skillet cover and increase the flame/stovetop to medium-high. Keep stirring frequently and continue cooking until the liquid has reduced to your desired thickness.

7. Serve.

    - Peperonata can be served with beef, pork, poultry, and fish.
    - You can also enjoy all of the remaining juices, either in the pan or on your plate.
    - Use some crusty Italian bread to soak up the remaining gravy on your plate. In Italy, we call this *la scarpetta*.

        Enjoy your delicious and simple Peperonata!

FROM TUSCANY WITH LOVE

LAURETTA AVINA

POLPETTE
(meatballs)

Recipe from Mara Marsalla Barsi-Perez (my mom)

Photo credit: Nino-P (iStock)

FROM TUSCANY WITH LOVE

Polpette is the official word for "Italian Meatballs," but do not expect to find spaghetti and meatballs on a menu in Italy. The idea of mixing meatballs with pasta started with Italian immigrants in the United States, who adapted their cuisine to the ingredients they found there during the great migration from 1880 to the early 1900s. Traditional Italian cuisine separates pasta and meat, a distinction that still surprises many non-Italians today.

Polpette brings back memories of my mom—my hero, my everything. She's the type of cook who could take a few simple ingredients and turn them into a feast. This recipe for Polpette is hers.

A bit about my mother. As I mentioned earlier, she was born in January of 1945, just months before WWII ended. She was born into a family of poor farmers in a small Italian village, Ponte a Moriano. Ponte a Moriano and many Italian villages were occupied by German soldiers. It was a struggle to survive during those years, but my mom's family's orchards, crops, and animals kept them fed.

And more on my grandfathers' storage space that I described earlier. My family had to guard what they had carefully. So, my grandfather and great-grandfather built a hidden pantry within the walls of their farmhouse, a secret refuge for staples like olive oil, wine, and cheese. The Nazis regularly plundered villages for food, leaving locals with nothing, so these precautions kept my mom and her family from dying of starvation.

Beyond tending their orchard and farms and protecting their food, the men also had to protect each other from being forcibly taken. The Nazis would ride into the small villages and would force able-bodied men into labor, so my grandfather and great-grandfather created another hideaway—a small crawlspace beneath the chicken coop, right under the manure, for hiding themselves. Young children kept watch at the edge of town, ready to run back and sound the alarm if Nazis approached. The men stayed hidden and safe thanks to their vigilance and the help of children although every day was a risk.

In Italian culture, it is common for multiple generations to share a home, and my mom lived in a farmhouse with her parents, siblings, grandparents, and great-grandparents all under the same roof. She learned to cook from my great-grandmother, Bisnonna Cecilia, who was very much a teacher and an untrained chef who created magic with food. I am so grateful that I was able to meet her and spend some years with her until we moved to Gilroy. What better way to keep alive Bisnonna Cecilia's memory than to share her recipes?

Recipe for Polpette

Ingredients

1 lb. of ground beef OR ½ lb. of ground beef and ½ lb. of ground pork

2–3 tablespoons of olive oil (more if needed)

3 cloves of garlic, pressed

2 tablespoons of fresh thyme, finely chopped

2 tablespoons of fresh oregano, finely chopped

3 eggs, beaten

1 teaspoon of nutmeg

Salt and pepper to taste

½ cup of grated Parmesan cheese

½ cup of grated Pecorino cheese

About 1 cup of seasoned (or unseasoned) breadcrumbs

1 cup of chicken or vegetable broth

2 tablespoons of flour

Directions

1. Prepare the Meat Mixture.

   - Add olive oil to a large skillet and warm it over medium heat.
   - Once hot, add the ground meat along with the pressed garlic, chopped thyme, chopped oregano, nutmeg, salt, and pepper.
   - Cook until the meat is fully cooked. Your Polpette should be a nice golden brown. Remove the cooked Polpette from the skillet and put it on a tray lined with paper towels to absorb any extra oil.

2. Make the Sauce.

    - While your meat and herbs are simmering, add the chicken or vegetable broth to a small saucepan.
    - Slowly add the flour and stir.
    - Cook over low heat until the sauce starts to thicken, then remove from heat and let it cool.
    - Your sauce should have a similar consistency to Biasciamella.

3. Combine ingredients.

    - Once the meat has cooled, add 2 of the beaten eggs to the meat mixture.
    - Stir in the prepared sauce and the grated Parmesan and Pecorino cheeses until everything is well combined.

4. Form the Meatballs.

    - Prepare a separate skillet with enough peanut oil for frying (about 1/2 inch deep).
    - Pour the breadcrumbs into a separate dish, and prepare the remaining beaten egg in a small bowl.
    - Take approx. 1 tablespoon of the meat mixture and roll it into a round ball.
    - Dredge each meatball in the beaten egg, then roll it in the breadcrumbs.
    - Continue forming meatballs until all the filling is used.

5. Fry the meatballs.

    - Once the oil is hot, carefully add the meatballs ensuring not to overcrowd the skillet.
    - Fry for 2-3 minutes, then flip and cook the other side.
    - The Polpette should have a golden to dark golden color when done.

6. Drain and serve.

    - Once cooked, remove the meatballs and place them on a plate lined with paper towels to absorb excess oil.
    - Serving suggestion:

- Serve the polpette as an appetizer, a side dish, or even in a meatball sandwich.
- They can also be enjoyed on top of pasta (though traditional Italians may disapprove!).
- Feel free to sauté them in spaghetti sauce if desired although this is more common in the U.S. than in Italy.

Enjoy your delicious homemade Polpette! They are sure to be a hit!

POMODORI RIPIENI CON TONNO

(Tomatoes filled with tuna)

Photo by Lauretta Avina

FROM TUSCANY WITH LOVE

For the most part, I don't like the taste of fish. However, I love this particular dish even though it also conjures up sad memories for me.

Summer, a season that I once loved, became a season I dreaded. It meant I would not see my mom much and would have more responsibilities. The thought gave me knots in my stomach. It also meant that I had to help care for my younger brother and sister.

I had to make sure the sink was clean, dishes were done after dinner, and other chores were completed. I only had a few friends to hang out with, and we rarely hung out, as many of them were not around during summer breaks. We did not have the money for summer vacations, extracurricular activities, summer camps, or lessons. We never really went on family vacations. I felt lonely during the summer breaks from school. The only other adult in the house was my father, who barely took an interest in raising us three kids. I came to hate this time of year, along with the Fall.

My mom also secured a fall job that usually started right after the cannery closed. It was at a walnut sorting and packaging business. As the walnut season rolled around, my mom worked double shifts sometimes if the seasons overlapped. She would finish her night shift at the cannery, sleep a few hours and head out again for her day shift. Her dedication left her exhausted, but she felt she had no other choice as she was the only stable breadwinner.

I am sure that my mom also felt incredibly overwhelmed, holding everything together with sheer determination. She did everything she could to provide for us, even when it must have taken every ounce of energy and strength to make it through each day. It could not have been easy, balancing work, her children's needs, learning a new language, and adjusting to a new life in a foreign country. Her resilience was her way of showing love, even in the face of exhaustion and frustration. Looking back, I see just how much weight she carried so we could survive.

During the day, one of my responsibilities was to keep my brother and sister quiet so she could sleep, even for a few hours. But, of course, that did not always go smoothly. One day, my brother snuck into her room, opened her eyes with his tiny fingers, and asked, "Sei sveglia?" ("Are you awake?")

Looking back, I realize that I had to grow up too fast in many ways. The negative experiences of being an Italian immigrant and the new reality of my life used to make me cry. It is a repercussion that still echoes inside me and has influenced, both consciously and unconsciously, some of the decisions I have made in my life.

Recipe for Pomodori Ripieni con Tonno

Ingredients

4 large beefsteak tomatoes (or any tomato variety you prefer)

1 can of tuna in olive oil, drained

1 generous tablespoon of capers, drained

1 small red onion, finely diced

4 tablespoons of mayonnaise

3 slices of any type of bread, soaked in vinegar (use this as the final step)

Wine vinegar or any preferred vinegar

Instructions

1. Prepare the filling.

    - In a large bowl, combine the drained tuna, diced onion, mayonnaise, and capers. Season with salt and pepper to taste.
    - Take the vinegar-soaked bread, gently squeeze to remove excess vinegar, and crumble it into the tuna mixture.

2. Blend the filling.

    - Use a whisk, spoon, or food processor to blend the filling. I prefer to use a food processor, and I pulse until I get the texture of the filling how I like it; not chunky but blended.
    - Put your filling dish in the refrigerator and let it sit overnight. By marinating overnight, the flavors will be more intense and better blended.

3. Prepare the tomatoes.

    - The next day, wash and pat dry the tomatoes.
    - Cut off the tops and carefully remove out the inner pulp to create a hollow shell.

4. Fill the tomatoes:

    - Spoon the tuna mixture into each tomato, pressing lightly to pack the filling.
    - Arrange the stuffed tomatoes on a serving tray and garnish each with parsley, an olive, or a basil leaf.

5. Serve.

    - This tomato and tuna dish must be served chilled.
    - If you find that your tomatoes are really large, and this recipe is not enough to fill all your tomatoes, just double the recipe.

    Don't like fish? Try this! You may change your mind!

FROM TUSCANY WITH LOVE

LAURETTA AVINA

RAPINI E SASICCIA ITALIANA

(Mustard Greens with Italian Sausage)

Photo by Lauretta Avina

FROM TUSCANY WITH LOVE

Many people do not know that mustard greens are not only edible but also incredibly nutritious. Mustard greens are loaded with micronutrients, fiber, and disease-fighting antioxidants. My favorite way to enjoy them is simply boiled, chopped, and sautéed with sausage, olive oil, and garlic.

Mustard greens carry a fascinating history. According to Britannica, mustard seeds were used as a spice as early as 3000 B.C., with mentions in ancient Indian and Sumerian texts. They were commonly referenced in Greek and Roman writings and even in the Bible, in the books of Matthew, Mark, and Luke.

Although I don't recall specific memories of eating or growing mustard greens in Italy, it's likely they appeared on our table without me even noticing. When we moved to Gilroy, California, my mom quickly realized she would need to adapt to the herbs, spices, and greens available locally to recreate our traditional Italian dishes. In the 1970s, mustard greens were not commonly found in grocery stores in our area. If you wanted them, you had to know where to look either by finding a friend who grew them, spotting wild patches, or looking for farmers who planted them as "green manure" to nourish the soil.

Our family's source for mustard greens? The hills, orchards, and fields around Gavilan College. Saturday outings became adventure-filled mustard-green harvesting trips led by my mom and aunt. They turned the trips into playful experiences with lots of giggling and laughter. I can still imagine how puzzled passersby must have looked, seeing a bunch of kids with two women deep in a muddy field. But those trips were more than foraging for mustard greens—they were for creating memories.

Recipe for Rapini e Salsiccia Italiana

Ingredients

4 large bunches of mustard greens, chopped

3 links of Italian sausage (without anise seeds), cut into small pieces — Lunardi's supermarket offers excellent authentic Italian sausage.

1/3 cup of olive oil

4 cloves garlic, finely chopped or crushed

1/2 cup of Chianti or Burgundy wine (optional, but adds a lovely depth of flavor)

Salt and pepper to taste

Directions

1. Prepare the mustard greens:

    - Wash the mustard greens well.
    - Add them to a large pot of boiling water.
    - Cook them until the stalks are tender.
    - Drain the greens and rinse with cold water to cool them down.
    - Once cool, take handfuls of the greens and squeeze out as much water as possible,
    - forming large balls. If you are not ready to use the mustard green balls, wrap them in freezer-appropriate saran wrap and freeze them for future use.

2. Cook the sausage and garlic.

    - In a large sauté pan, add olive oil and heat it over medium heat.
    - Add garlic and chopped sausage to the pan.
    - Cook for about 5 minutes, stirring occasionally.

3. Combine and cook.

    - As the garlic and sausage are cooking, chop the mustard greens.
    - Add the chopped mustard greens to the skillet and stir well.
    - Add red wine (Chianti) to the skillet and continue cooking while stirring occasionally to reduce the wine.
    - Ensure the sausage is thoroughly cooked and the wine has reduced sufficiently.

4. Finish and serve.

> - If needed, add more olive oil to create a yummy sugo (sauce).
> - This dish can be paired with steak, pork loin roast, or chicken.
> - It can also be served on top of polenta.

5. Serve with crusty Italian bread to soak up the flavorful sauce.

> *Enjoy this delicious, different, and nutritious winter dish!*

FROM TUSCANY WITH LOVE

RISOTTO CON FUNGHI

Photo credit: ReDunn Lev (iStock)

FROM TUSCANY WITH LOVE

Ah, risotto con funghi! One of my favorite risottos! I do not associate this recipe with any one Italian family or friend, but I do with porcini mushrooms. They remind me of my maternal uncle, Zio Beppino, and his daughter, my first cousin, Michela. Zio Beppino and Michela are experts in identifying and gathering porcini mushrooms. Whenever I go to Italy, Michela always sends me home with a large bag of dried porcini that she or my uncle have gathered.

During the summer of 2022, I stayed with Michela for a few days, and she made me Porcini Mushroom Soup. It was so good. I had never eaten a soup made only with porcini mushrooms before. I could eat porcini mushrooms every day. The prime season to gather porcini in Tuscany is mid-September to late October.

The best place to find porcini is at the foot of chestnut and pine trees after some rain. When the sun shines after the rain, the damp, warm conditions create the ideal environment for porcini. I have photos of my cousins holding up giant-sized porcini, reveling in their unexpected success at finding such large specimens.

Risotto con funghi is not a dish that you can prepare ahead of time because risotto is best served fresh. Here is how you make it:

Recipe for Risotto con Funghi

Ingredients

4 Tbsp. of butter - divided

4 Tbsp. Extra Virgin Olive Oil

4 garlic cloves - diced or pressed

16 oz package of whole mushrooms, rinsed, drained, and sliced.

1/2 cup dry white wine. If you do not have wine in the house do not worry, your risotto will still come out delicious.

1 yellow onion - chopped

1 + 1/2 cups of Arborio Rice

32-ounces of Chicken Broth or Stock, more or less, depending on how much rice you use.

1 + 1/2 tsp. salt

1/4 cup Parmigiano-Reggiano cheese grated, and extra for serving

Instructions

1. Prepare the rice.

    - Use a 5qt - 8qt stock pot. (I prefer using a bigger one rather than a smaller one).
    - Coat the bottom of the pan with olive oil and turn on your stovetop.
    - As soon as the pot is hot enough, add the arborio rice.
    - Toast the arborio rice for about 2 minutes, constantly stirring as it toasts.
    - Add the garlic and sliced onions and continue to sauté all the ingredients, stirring constantly to prevent burning, until the onion becomes a bit translucent, about 2-3 minutes.

2. Add the remainder of the ingredients.

    - Add the wine, broth, and diced/chopped porcini mushrooms, continuously stirring.
    - It is important to keep the rice constantly covered with hot broth. I use a ladle (one ladle at a time) to add either water or additional broth to the pot, as I find this method easier to measure how much extra liquid I add. You can tell if the risotto needs more liquid if it starts to stick to the bottom of the pan or you see that the broth has been absorbed.
    - It is crucial to keep stirring as the risotto cooks. During the cooking process, the risotto will cook and absorb the liquid quickly, and it may start to stick to the bottom of the pan.
    - It usually takes about 15-20 minutes for the rice to be done. Your rice should not be completely dry of liquid; it should look and feel moist.

3. Complete the last step: *mantecatura*.

> ➤ One last step before you serve it: add the butter and parmesan cheese and stir until well blended. This is called "Mantecatura," which means creaming the risotto with butter and cheese.

4. Serve.

> ➤ Your risotto is now ready to be served.
>
> ➤ I usually have fresh parmesan cheese on the dinner table for those who would like to add extra cheese to their serving.

FROM TUSCANY WITH LOVE

SFORMATO
String Bean Flan

FROM TUSCANY WITH LOVE

This recipe brings back loving memories of my great-aunt Yolanda, whom we all lovingly called Landa. Apart from my mom, Landa was everything to me—my second mother. She was a non-cloistered nun who took care of all the household needs for her brother, Giuseppe Marsalla, a priest whom I called Zio Beppe. Nestled in my heart are the countless weeks I spent with them in Italy.

My mom had four children in total. I'm the eldest, followed by Franchina, who was born in 1965 with a cleft palate. Tragically, after surgery to repair her palate when she was just two years old, she never woke up from anesthesia. I was only three at the time, but I have vivid memories of her. I remember the day my parents returned home from the hospital without her. When I asked where Franchina was, my mom knelt down and gently told me that the angels had taken her to heaven because they needed her help. While I do not recall my feelings then, I distinctly remember standing by her grave at her funeral. Another bittersweet memory is when I accidentally smashed Franchina's finger at Landa and Beppe's house. My mom was understandably angry and protective, so I hid under the kitchen table, but Landa came to my defense.

After Franchina, my mom faced two more difficult pregnancies. Both pregnancies resulted in my mother suffering severe hemorrhaging. Doctors advised her not to have more children if she wanted to live. During her last pregnancy with my brother, she was hospitalized for a month.

During these two pregnancies and the aftermath and to give my mother a helping hand, Zio Beppe would pick me up and I would live with them for weeks. I would follow both around like a shadow, but more so my Zio Beppe. I was the apple of his eye, and he was mine. He even made me an altar "boy" during mass when girls were not allowed to serve.

My mom kept my hair short so I could pass as a boy. When I trailed behind Zia Landa, I would be mesmerized by her grace as she did laundry—not at a laundromat, but at the local river with homemade soap. I thought she had magical powers as I watched her balance baskets of laundry, vegetables, and fruit on her head, briskly walking uphill toward the church and home, never once losing her balance, or dropping a basket.

Realizing that I should have some friends around my age, my Zio surprised me on my next extended stay. He collaborated with my cousin Vittorio from Pavia—a suburb of Milan—to install a swing in the backyard of the home in Cocciglia and placed 3' statues of Snow White and the Seven Dwarfs in the small backyard grotto. When I arrived, I was ecstatic to see it, and it quickly became a favorite spot for all the children in Cocciglia. I also spent hours having imaginary conversations and adventures with those beautifully crafted statues, and to this day, Snow White remains one of my favorite princesses, along with Cinderella.

Atop the second and highest grotto, he placed a tall statue of the Immaculate Conception, standing majestically against the backdrop of the granite and looking down on the back gardens. The Immaculate Conception to this day, for me, is exactly what our holy mother should look like. The image of the Immaculate Conception became engrained in my mind and spirit after watching the 1943 movie about St. Bernadette, *The Song of Bernadette*, starring Jennifer Jones. This movie captured my seven-year-old heart to an extent that I still find difficult to articulate. All that I can say is that St. Bernadette became my favorite saint, inspiring me to choose her name at my Confirmation.

Adding to the enchantment, Zio Beppe placed statues of Santa Claus and Bambi along the walkway from the house to the fence at the end of the yard. The memories of Zio Beppe and Zia Landa's backyard, filled with swings, statues, and grottos, are among my most cherished childhood moments. I felt so loved.

Every time I return to Italy, I drive to Cocciglia, park in the small piazza, and walk the cobblestone path, to the very top where the Church and house I used to live in with Zio Beppe and Zia Landa are located. As I walk up the cobblestone path, I am overtaken by the breathtaking panorama of the valley below, the ancient architecture surrounding me, and the green hills adorned with vibrant green pine trees and other foliage. Cocciglia feels like the perfect backdrop for a medieval movie, walking up the cobblestone path feels as if you are walking in a scene of *Game of Thrones*.

Though I cannot enter the yard anymore since it is fenced and locked, I know my Snow White, the Dwarfs, Bambi, Santa Claus, and my swing are all still there, as if patiently awaiting my return. If it were not for the obvious aging caused by time, I would say that it is as if time had stopped for them preserving the precious moments just as I remembered. I can still hear the echoes of laughter and feel the love of our family gatherings. I close my eyes and imagine the scent of freshly made Ravioli that used to linger in the air; now they are evanescent memories from my childhood.

Every visit stirs a deep nostalgia, and I cannot help but cry. My husband and I spent Christmas of 2019 in Italy. During our visit, my wonderful cousin Michela surprised me with the key to the church and the house. She had found the curator and managed to secure the key. When she shared the good news, my heart skipped a beat, then quickened with excitement as I realized that after 47 years, I would finally have the chance to walk within the walls that had once held so much love and countless cherished memories for me.

As I stepped through the front door, I cautiously take a step, trying to capture every second of the experience as I am suddenly transformed into the eight-year-old little girl that once lived here. My heart and mind remembered the layout of the house so well that I did not even have to tell my legs where to walk; my feet remembered every path. The echoes of long-past conversations and laughter embedded in the walls followed me, wrapping around me in a warm embrace. As I eased out of my transformation, my adult eyes take in the house. What I once thought was a palace was now smaller, a normal-sized home.

Continuing down the short hallway past the study, to the left, is the entrance to the kitchen. The kitchen had an entrance to the study as well, and this is where I remember running away from my Zio Beppino (my mom's brother) because he was going to give me a haircut and I was scared he would cut my ears off. I heard myself chuckling out loud at the memory. From the kitchen window on the south end of the room, I could look down on the whole village and valley. The house sat so high up from the bottom of the village that when I looked out the window it felt like I was hovering in the air, as if I could fly. Down the hallway from the kitchen, again to the left, was the bathroom, where, sadly, my great-grandfather passed away.

Of course, the kitchen was the grandest room, the center of the house that made everything so homey. My soul and heart embracing the vivid memories, the warmth, love, and tradition that was celebrated in this kitchen is more than I can bear. How many dreams had I had throughout the years of coming back and still finding Landa in the kitchen? Too many to count. In some way, I could feel the echo of her spirit circling the room, gently touching my heart as if it were trying to comfort me. Landa's small square table still stood as if waiting for Zia Landa to walk back in and start making her tordelli. My heart swelled with overwhelming emotions as I took it all in. My eyes welled up with joyful tears along with the realization that the moments I experienced with Zia Landa and Zio Beppe in this home and in Cocciglia are in the past and can no longer be relived. The intensity of these feelings caused me to cry so hard that my shoulders shook. My tears were the only way that I could release the intensity of the happiness and nostalgia that I felt.

Sadly, about ten years ago, the church rented the home to a French couple who were hoarders and ended up damaging the house so that presently, it is not habitable. After evicting them, the church found itself faced with a property that now needs complete restoration. Perhaps, one day, the church will allow someone to restore the house to its former glory.

The church itself was also in disarray, with mice droppings, cobwebs, and dust blanketing everything. Sadly, the church is now barely used for mass but for a couple of times a year. How sad! It is a beautiful, ancient church-built centuries ago. Yet, I could not help but envision how magnificent it could be again with a thorough cleaning. As I stood inside the church, memories flooded back of the times Landa and I attended mass there every day at 12 noon. I closed my eyes and could vividly picture her sitting to my right, gently reminding me to settle down when my excitement got the better of me.

Those moments felt frozen in time, a cherished connection to a past that seemed just out of reach. I kept thinking that if I were younger, I would approach the church leaders and offer to buy the house. It would make an ideal place for destination weddings and other celebrations along with making a perfect place to film a movie.

The moments I spent with Zia Landa and Zio Beppe are some of the happiest memories of my life and of living in Italy. Despite the ache of missing them, my love for Zia Landa and Zio Beppe is a constant reminder of the deep and lasting impact they had on my life. (For those interested in the history of Cocciglia, I have provided a link with more information about this special place in the references.

LAURETTA AVINA

Recipe for Sformato di Fagiolini

Recipe by Mara Marsalla Barsi-Perez

Ingredients

2 lbs. green beans, cooked, drained and chopped

Besciamella sauce (see Besciamella recipe)

2 eggs

1/2 cup grated Romano cheese

3 tbsp chopped parsley

3 tbsp chopped thyme

1/2 cup chicken livers, chopped and sauteed

1/2 teaspoon of nutmeg

salt and pepper to taste

Directions

1. Prepare.

    - Grease and flour a souffle dish or mold.
    - Mix all the ingredients. (Nota bene: There are different variations. You can substitute any other vegetable for string beans. You can use sausage, bacon, or hamburger in place of the chicken livers.)
    - Pour into the greased souffle dish.

2. Cook.

    - Place the dish in a pre-heated oven (350 degrees).
    - Bake for about one hour.
    - At one hour, insert a knife in the center; if it comes out clean (not wet with ingredients) the souffle is done.

What a great way to eat green beans!

References

https://bellabagnidilucca.com/2012/12/19/cocciglia/

https://bellabagnidilucca.com/2020/07/22/a-walk-in-cocciglia-and-pallegio/

VELLUTATA

Photo by Lauretta Avina

This recipe takes me back to the fields and hills surrounding San Pancrazio, where the sweet fragrance of blooming tiglio trees mingled with the warmth of summer nights as I chased fireflies. San Pancrazio sits between two smaller towns, blending seamlessly with no clear borders, all surrounded by beautiful villas—Villa Saltocchio, Villa Oliva, Villa Grabau, and Villa Reale.

Villa Oliva, now considered a historic estate (dating to the 16th charm), of which my home was a small part, will always be special among my memories. As a child, I never realized the historical significance of my growing-up place. I just loved its charm, the manicured gardens and forest setting, and the peaceful beauty I saw outside my bedroom window every day when I woke up, did my homework, or went to bed.

To be fair to all the other beautiful villas, I have included links to information about them, with photos, in the reference list. You must admit: Tuscany is clearly a place to be loved!

And now, here is the recipe for Vellutata, a dish that brings Tuscany to mind. This recipe is perfect for using zucchini, especially if your garden overflows with it. It can be served warm or cold, but when I eat Vellutata, I prefer it warm with grated parmesan cheese and optional croutons, finished with a drizzle of olive oil. Italians often drizzle olive oil over their soups—Minestrone, Vellutata, Farinata, and many others. Without it, my soup feels incomplete.

Recipe for Vellutata

Ingredients

4 large zucchini, chopped

1 yellow onion, chopped

2 containers vegetable or chicken broth

1 vegetable bouillon cube (optional, for added flavor)

Instructions

1. Cook the vegetables.

   > In a large pot, add the chopped zucchini, onion, and vegetable broth (or substitute with any broth or water and bouillon for flavor).

   > Bring the pot to a boil, then reduce the heat to a simmer. Cook until the zucchini is very tender, about 15-20 minutes—make sure not to undercook.

2. Blend to make a smooth bisque.

   > Once the zucchini and onion are cooked, transfer them to a blender.

   > Add about 1/3 to 1/2 cup of the cooking broth and blend until smooth and velvety.

   > Add more broth as needed to reach your preferred consistency, saving any remaining broth for another use.

3. Optional add-ins.

   > If you'd like a heartier version, add cooked barley, tortellini, or farro to the Vellutata. You may need to add extra broth, as these ingredients will absorb some liquid. Start with a small amount, adding more broth as needed.

4. Serve.

   > Depending on your preference, Zucchini Vellutata can be enjoyed hot or cold.

   > It can be served as an appetizer in small cups or as a starter.

   > This simple soup is delicious on its own, but feel free to experiment with garnishes like a drizzle of olive oil, a sprinkle of Parmesan, or a few fresh basil leaves.

Enjoy!

References

Villa Reale-https://villarealedimarlia.it/en/
Villa Oliva-https://www.villaoliva.it/en/
Villa Grabau- https://www.villagrabau.it/en/the-villa/

ABOUT THE AUTHOR

Lauretta Avina

Lauretta Avina, an Italian American immigrant, has a deep passion for sharing good food with family and friends. She self-published her first cookbook, *Ricette del Mio Paese*, in 2011. At the time of publication, Lauretta had been married for 36 years to her husband, a 24-year Army Veteran, now retired.

Lauretta is the founder and president of the Franca Barsi Memorial Scholarship, created to honor her late sister by awarding a scholarship annually to a graduating high school senior. Following her sister's tragic death due to domestic violence, Lauretta became a dedicated advocate and volunteer, educating others about domestic violence prevention and services. She has served as a guest speaker for various social welfare agencies and juvenile probation Victim Awareness Classes.

In addition to her advocacy for domestic violence victims, Lauretta is a staunch supporter of military veterans and their families. She also advocates for students in her role as a Guidance Technician at her local high school.

When she has time, Lauretta enjoys preparing delicious meals, often using vegetables and spices from her husband's garden. She is well-known in her community for her

Lasagna alla Lucchese and her biscotti, which are frequently requested and sometimes sold to help fund her sister's memorial scholarship.

Despite not being a formally trained chef, Lauretta cooks from the heart, preparing what she loves to eat. Fluent in her native Italian, she keeps her language skills sharp through frequent trips to Italy to visit family and friends.

Lauretta's contributions have earned her numerous awards, including honors from the U.S. Army, the California Army National Guard, the Santa Clara County Juvenile Probation-Victim Services, and the American Legion Post 69. She is also a member of the Golden Key International Honour Society.

Throughout her life, Lauretta has dedicated countless volunteer hours to the California Army National Guard Family Readiness Group, especially during the 1989 Loma Prieta earthquake, as well as to the Veterans of Foreign Wars, including serving as M.C. for the Veterans Day Parade. Additionally, she has also volunteered for the Gilroy Garlic Festival, at her sons' elementary, middle school and high school and was briefly a board member for Emmaus House, a shelter for domestic violence female victims and their children.

Her community involvement extends beyond advocacy; Lauretta has held several pageant titles, including Miss Gilroy Bonanza Days 1982, Miss Gilroy Garlic 1983, and Miss Gavilan Hills Scholarship Pageant 1985. She was also 2nd runner-up in the Mrs. California USA pageant and has judged pageants at both the local and state levels.

In her spare time, Lauretta enjoys long walks with her two dogs, Ava and Pepper, and her husband. She loves swimming, beach outings, crafting, and most of all, singing.

Photo with my classmates and teacher, June 1972:

Select MSI Press LLC Publications

Books with recipes

Dia de Muertos

From Tuscany with Love (Avina)

Girl, You Got This! (Renz)

Syrian Folktales (M. Imady)

Immigrant lives

From Tuscany with Love

Good Blood (Schaffer)

Language and cultural books

Achieving Nativelike Second Language Proficiency (Leaver)

Communicative Focus (Shekhtman and Kupchanka)

Damascus amid the War (M. Imady)

How to Improve Your Foreign Language Immediately (Shekhtman)

Individualized Study Plans for Very Advanced Students of Foreign Languages (Leaver)

Journal for Distinguished Language Studies (Zhou and Brinton)

Practices That Work: Bringing Learners to Professional Levels of Proficiency in World Languages (Garza)

The Invisible Foreign Language Classroom (Dabbs & Leaver)

The Rise and Fall of Muslim Civil Society (O. Imady)

Think Yourself into Becoming a Language Learning Super Star (Leaver)

When You're Shoved from the Right, Look to Your Left (O. Imady)

Working with Advanced Foreign Language Students (Shekhtman)

Memoirs

Blest Atheist (Mahlou)

Forget the Goal, the Journey Counts (Stites)

From Deep Within (Lewis)

GodSway (Keathley)

Lamentations of the Heart (Wells-Smith)

Las Historias de Mi Vida (Ustman)

Road to Damascus (E. Imady)

Since Sinai (Gonyou)